SIMPLE SERMONS
on the
TEN COMMANDMENTS

SIMPLE SERMONS
on the
TEN COMMANDMENTS

by
W. HERSCHEL FORD, B.A., D.D.

INTRODUCTION BY
DR. ROBERT G. LEE

ZONDERVAN PUBLISHING HOUSE
GRAND RAPIDS, MICHIGAN

SIMPLE SERMONS ON THE TEN COMMANDMENTS
Copyright 1956 by
Zondervan Publishing House
Grand Rapids, Michigan

First printing — 1956
Second printing — 1957
Third printing — 1959
Fourth printing — 1964

Printed in the United States of America

FOREWORD

These Simple Sermons on the Ten Commandments were preached in the First Baptist Church of El Paso, Texas. I thank God for the privilege of serving as pastor of this · wonderful church and am grateful for the help its members give me in the publication and distribution of these books.

The material for these sermons was gathered from many sources — sources too numerous for me to mention, but I thank all those whose writings have helped me to prepare these messages.

My preacher brethren are certainly welcome to use these sermons in any way that will bring glory to God and souls to the Savior.

W. HERSCHEL FORD

INTRODUCTION

When Dr. S. D. Gordon wrote many books on the general title *Quiet Talks*, he blessed the world. Dr. Herschel Ford, pastor of the great First Baptist Church, El Paso, Texas, has blessed hundreds of thousands with his books published under the general title *Simple Sermons*.

With delight, with spiritual profit, and with much gratitude for the many books by this faithful and God-used servant of Christ, I have read the manuscript *Simple Sermons on the Ten Commandments*. Pungent, potent, frequently profound rather than just simple, and practical are these sermons in their urge for men to put God first and to follow Him fully.

Inspiringly informative and filled with impressive illustrations and truths, ancient and up-to-date, that soberly warn the mind and woo the heart, these sermons urge men to be obedient to the commandments. They also teach that the Ten Commandments are not the ghostly whisper of a dead age, but are as authoritative for our day as they were authoritative when they were given in writing by the Lord on tables of stone centuries ago (Exodus 24:16).

Informative in an unusual way, with words weighty and winsome, these sermons set forth the holiness of God, the retributive providence of God, the demands of God for obedience, the rewards of God guaranteed to the obedient, and the goodness of God that should lead all men everywhere to repentance and to service.

INTRODUCTION

All who read, teach, preach, or live out these most excellent "simple sermons" will find themselves the beneficiaries of Dr. Ford's thought, study and scholarship.

ROBERT G. LEE

Memphis, Tennessee

CONTENTS

Sermon 1

NO OTHER GODS BEFORE ME

Thou shalt have no other gods before me (Exodus 20:3).

The children of Israel were on their way to the Promised Land. God was going to make of them a great nation. He was going to settle them in a land flowing with milk and honey. Now a country cannot be run without rules and laws, so God had Moses gather all Israel before Mount Sinai and there He gave them the Law. He gave them what we call the Ten Commandments. One modern preacher calls these commandments "The Ten Rules for Living."

Sometime ago I went into a new court house in one of the county seat towns of North Carolina. Directly behind the Judge's bench I saw the Ten Commandments engraved on two beautiful marble slabs._ I remembered that the laws of our nation are based upon the Ten Commandments.

Life is different today from what it was in Moses' day and many people say that the Ten Commandments are out of date. But God is always the same and His principles and natural laws are eternal. About 175 years ago a group of wise men framed the Constitution of the United States. These laws were well adapted to the life of that time, yet, although our country has seen many great changes, this Constitution, with a few amendments, is still satisfactory to guide our nation. It is the same with the Ten Commandments which God has given to us. Yes, today we are modern. Our life is far ahead of Moses' time. Yet the same basic principles which guided Israel apply to American life today.

Some people today say that the Gospel has displaced the law. They say that we live entirely under grace and that the law has nothing to do with us. But Jesus said, "Think not that I am come to destroy the law, or the prophets: I am not come to destroy but to fulfill. For verily I say unto you, Till heaven and earth pass, one jot or one tittle shall in no wise pass from the law, till all be fulfilled" (Matt. 5:17, 18).

A man and his colored servant went deep-sea fishing one night. Late that night as they were making their way toward the shore, the man became sleepy and turned the wheel of the boat over to his servant. He pointed out the North Star to the servant, told him to keep his eye fixed on that star and thus he would find his way home. The man went to sleep, but pretty soon Mose awakened him, crying out in excitement: "Boss, wake up and show me another star. I have done run clean past that one." Many people feel that way about the Ten Commandments, but you can't run past them any more than you can run past the North Star. These are God's unchangeable laws and you can't ignore them without disaster.

The purpose of the moral law is to show God's standard of perfection. The law shows a man what he is and what he ought to be. The law is a mirror, showing us our sins and how far we are falling short of God's purpose for our lives. As a man looks into the law, he says, "I am guilty of this. I am guilty of that." Seeing his guilt he then says, "I must do something about it." Galatians 3:24 tells us that the law is a schoolmaster to bring us to Christ. The law shows us that we are sinful and that we need the cleansing blood of the Lord Jesus. We must remember that God in the Commandments is not speaking simply to a nation, but to individuals as well. He says, "Thou shalt," and "Thou shalt not." In the Ten Commandments God is talking to you and me.

I. THE FIRST COMMANDMENT GIVEN

God begins by saying, "I am the Lord thy God." There is a strong note of authority here. He reminds Israel that He found them in slavery, freed them, brought them out and is going to give them a new and wonderful home. Therefore He had a right to ask them to do certain things and to refrain from doing other things. Now God puts it straight — "Thou shalt have no other gods before me." Actually He is saying, "I am to be your only God."

Israel had been in Egypt and there had seen a multiplicity of gods. Soon they would be in Canaan where they would find nations with many other gods. Now the Lord says, "You will have nothing to do with them. They are dead idols. I am the living God."

If we follow the history of Israel we find that the people violated this first commandment. There came a time when God was forgotten and the Israelites worshiped the gods of the nations round about them. God had to send them into captivity before they learned their lesson. Now today, the Jews are strong on this idea of the One True God. . . . So God spoke out, saying, "Thou shalt have no other gods before me." He is still saying the same thing today.

II. LET US LOOK AT SOME GROSS IDOLATRY

Man is incurably religious. The religious instinct has been planted deep within his nature. He has a desire to look up to some eternal source of power and help. If he doesn't know the One True God, he makes a god and bows down before it.

Go back hundreds of years and you will find that even the nations which were noted for their science and art were guilty of the grossest idolatry. The Greeks had thirty thousand gods. These gods were represented as having husbands and wives and engaging in the most immoral practices. When Paul went to Athens, he found gods on every corner, gods in the homes, gods in the gardens, gods everywhere. Then, fearing that they might miss some god, they erected a statue "to the unknown god." Down through the ages, men have worshiped the sun, the moon, the stars. Some worship the rivers, the groves, the birds, the fishes. The people in India today are starving for meat, while thousands of cows roam their streets. However, they can't kill them because they believe them to be sacred. They worship them as gods. All over the world today men bow down to man-made idols.

Some years ago I attended the World's Fair in Chicago. An Asiatic temple had been brought to Chicago and set up on the Fair grounds. In this temple there were many idols and many gods. The guide who conducted us through the temple made this explanation, "The people pray to this god when they want a good crop. They pray to this god for health and to this one for wealth. A woman who wants children prays to this god." Oh, the sorrow of it! The sorrow of men bowing down before helpless gods of wood and stone, while the great living God of heaven is always standing ready to help those who call upon Him.

III. Let Us Think Now of Refined Idolatry

The people of America are refined and cultured. They do not bow down before the statue of Buddha, nor pray to a god of wood or stone. Are they therefore innocent? Have they kept the first commandment perfectly? No, they are just as guilty as all the others — their idolatry is just a bit more refined.

1. *Some worship the god of nature.* On the Lord's Day many Americans do not come to the House of God and seek a new touch with the Lord. We find them on the golf course, by a fishing stream, or taking a journey to the mountains. They say, "We can worship God just as well on the golf course as in the church." The trouble is that they don't worship Him there. They are not thinking of God when they are playing golf. They are thinking of making a long drive or getting their golf ball out of the rough.

Nature is grand and wonderful to enjoy. God has given it to us for our own pleasure, but we are not to worship the creation instead of the Creator. Can nature help you in the time of need? Can nature comfort your heart in sorrow? Can nature walk with you through the valley of the shadow? No, but God can.

A soldier tells of a fierce battle in Virginia during the War between the States. Just a few feet of earth separated the men of the North from the men of the South. The boys in blue and the boys in grey stood face to face for hours in deadly combat. When the battle was over, this soldier's company was assigned to the burial detail. He said that in a very small area they collected sixteen hundred bodies. Yet the next morning nature smiled down upon the scene. The birds sang in the trees, the flowers bloomed by the wayside, even the soil had been enriched by the blood of these men. Nature didn't care; she was not concerned. I am not going to worship such a god. I want to worship One who is concerned about me.

James Oliver Curwood wrote many wonderful stories of nature and outdoor life. He said, "When I come down to die, I will be content to have the flowers, the trees and the grass around me." Oh, my friends, I want more than that when I come down to die. I want Jesus to be there. I want to feel the touch of his hand on mine as my feet touch the icy waters of the river of death. I want to hear Him say, "I am with you. I will take you across the river, I will take you Home."

2. *Some worship the god of health.* I remember a young man of another day who was always boasting about his big muscles and his big, strong body. Yet he had no moral strength. He was untrue to his wife and let immorality ruin him. Health is a wonderful gift of God. We ought to improve it as much as we can, but we are not to be a slave to it. If on Sunday morning you say, "For the sake of my health I will stay in bed this morning and not go to church," you are worshiping the wrong god.

Many people are strong enough and well enough to go to work every day and go out to some place of amusement every night. But when Sunday comes, they have the "Sunday sickness." They can't go to church on Sunday morning and on Sunday night they say, "It isn't best for me to go out tonight." We should give attention to our health. We should have a physical check-up from time to time. We should take the medicine prescribed for us, but we are not to put the god of health before the God of heaven.

3. *Some worship the god of sports.* Certainly we would not condemn all sports — most of us love to watch a good game. But some are so enthusiastic about sports that all else is forgotten. The sports page is devoured and the Bible is neglected. The heroes of the diamond and the gridiron are more familiar to them than the great men of the Bible. While there may be no harm in many of these games, there is harm when we desecrate the Lord's Day by attending

them. There is harm in them when we spend money for sports which rightly belongs to God. There is harm in them when we place sports above God in our affections.

4. *Some worship the god of science and learning.* Tremendous strides have been made in scientific research in the past few decades. The slumbering forces of nature have been discovered and used for the benefit of mankind. But we are in danger of trusting science and human wisdom and forgetting God. Most of modern science has in it no room for God or prayer. When the doctor goes to the operating room he has at his disposal all the modern discoveries to add to his own skill. But he needs something else; he needs the help of God. He needs to pray that God will put His Big Hand over the surgeon's hand. In every scientific endeavor we still need the help of God.

The things of science which are believed true today are discarded as error tomorrow. A textbook on science ten years old is out of date. Paul was right when he said, "Whether there be knowledge it shall vanish." Human learning, human knowledge and human wisdom pass away. Only God remains forever the same.

5. *Some worship the god of pleasure.* The Bible speaks of people who are "lovers of pleasure more than lovers of God." Our American life is geared to the idea of pleasure. Every advertisement, every radio and every television set screams out that you can find happiness in the pleasures of the world. A special appeal is made to our young people. Consequently thousands of them renounce all allegiance to God and follow the god of pleasure. I am not against pleasure that is clean and fine and uplifting, but I am against any form of pleasure which weans our people away from God.

A preacher was holding a revival in a certain church. On Monday night three young people came forward confessing

Christ. On Tuesday night two more came forward and on Wednesday night there were six who confessed the Savior. The preacher wondered what was the secret of this moving of the Spirit, but it was later in the week before he found out. In the church there was a beautiful and popular girl who was a captain in her training group. She wanted to have a good program on Sunday night, so she gave out the various parts and worked hard on the program all the week. On Saturday afternoon one of her friends called and invited her to be one of a group of young people who would spend the weekend at the beach. She wanted to go, but she knew that her duty lay with her church and her training group, so she declined the invitation. Her friends told her what a fool she was. Nobody would be at the training group meeting anyway, since six of them were going away. But on Sunday night when she arrived at church she was surprised to find the other young people who had gone to the beach. This is what they said to her: "Oh, Virginia, we had a miserable trip. We didn't enjoy the beach yesterday and this morning we decided that we would all come back in time for the meeting and church tonight." It was not surprising that these six young people were the first to accept Christ in the meeting. But here is the awful question: What if Virginia had left her place of duty and gone on this pleasure trip? These other young people would never have been impressed with her religion or her church. Ah, the pleasures of the world last for but a little while. The zest soon dies out. But the greatest pleasure of all is found in faithful service to the Lord.

6. *Some worship the god of popularity*. Oh, how some Christians love to shine! They like to get their names and pictures in the paper. They love the pre-eminence. They love to stand high in the opinion of the world.

The sinner prefers the favor of man to the favor of God.

He is careful how his character stands in the eyes of men, but he doesn't care how he stands in the eyes of God. Men often do the things which they know to be displeasing to God, in order to secure the favor of their fellow men. It is a tragic thing when men set greater value on the favor of man than on the favor of God.

Jesus talked about people who did things to be seen of men. He said that they would have their reward. What was this reward? It was simply the notice of men. But I want to tell you that this is not the greatest reward. Today many of our church members are elected to worldly positions; they work hard for honors; they want public notice; they have their reward, but it is not the best reward. The best reward comes from God, for the service which we render Him. Someday He will say, "Well done." He will give out His rewards in heaven. But these will be for the work done for Him and His Church. The God of heaven is certainly better than the god of popularity and acclaim.

7. *Some worship the god of wealth.* Our coins bear the inscription, "In God we trust." But thousands of people are putting their trust in the almighty dollar instead of the Almighty God. In this complex life we must have some money, but when we rely on silver and gold, when our chief goal in life is to get more money, when we put gold above God, we are in great danger. Money in itself can be a useful thing; it can be used to bless man and glorify God. But when money masters you, when you love it more than God, you are in great danger.

Many church members spend money on everything in the world, and have little or none for God's work. I do not say it, but the Bible says that you are robbing God. He makes it possible for you to get money and at least a tenth of your income belongs to Him. I would not like to be hailed before a court and have someone say, "This man robbed his neighbor." But this would be better than to be forced to stand someday before the judgment seat of Christ and have it said that I robbed God!

A certain man had much money and a large estate. Hundreds of visitors came to see his home and his garden. A special servant showed them over the grounds. One day a man asked, "How much is this estate worth?" The servant answered, "I don't know how much it is worth, but I do know how much it cost the owner — it cost him his soul." Oh, listen to Jesus as He says, "For what shall it profit a man, if he shall gain the whole world, and lose his own soul?"

Today the world is full of practical atheists and many of them are in our churches. They would never dare say with their lips, "There is no God," but their conduct proclaims this belief every day. They violate God's commands, they desecrate His day, they ignore His Church — they live as if there were no God. In the Great Day of Judgment God will say, "Depart from me, ye cursed, into everlasting fire."

I tell you that we should never have any other god than the God of heaven. He is the only One who can help us in the time of need, in the time of sorrow, in the time when the death angel comes knocking at the door. Suppose that sorrow should come to you tomorrow. Suppose that your loved one should die: your heart would be broken; your money could not comfort you then; your pleasure, your popularity, your learning, none of these could help you. But Jesus can help you. He says, I know what sorrow is. I went through all that you are experiencing. I will not leave you, I will be with you and cause every thing to work out for your good. Let not your heart be troubled.

> Does Jesus care when I've said "goodbye"
> To the dearest on earth to me,

And my sad heart aches
Till it nearly breaks,
Is it aught to Him, does He see?

O yes, He cares, I know He cares,
His heart is touched with my grief;
When the days are weary,
The long nights dreary,
I know my Savior cares.

Someday you will come to the river of death. The doctor will whisper, "He can't last much longer." Your loved ones will stand around weeping. You are going to need some help then. Will it help you to know that you have made lots of money? Will it help to know that you have been popular, or learned? No, when you come to the end of your way the only thing that will help you will be to remember that the God of heaven was your God and Father, and that the Christ of the Cross was your Savior.

But let me tell you that God is not your Father until you have come to Him through faith in the Lord Jesus Christ. The Bible makes this very plain. Someone says, "But I am keeping the Ten Commandments." If you are not a Christian, if you have not accepted Christ as your Savior, you are not even keeping the first commandment. For if you love God and put Him first, surely you will not reject the Son whom He gave to die for you on Calvary. The only way for you to even make a start toward keeping the first commandment is by leaving your sin and trusting Christ as your Savior.

A boy went to Chicago to become a student at the Moody Bible Institute. He secured a part-time job in a warehouse to pay his school expenses. A worldly young man worked beside him. One day the Christian boy told the worldling that he wished he would give up his sin and let Jesus come into his heart. The other boy laughed, reached into his pocket and drew out a roll of bills. Holding up this money, he said, "This is all the Jesus Christ I want." A few minutes later there was an accident in the warehouse and these two young men were crushed to death beneath the freight elevator. One young man went out into eternity, loving and serving Jesus; the the other young man went toward the judgment, holding on to his money and saying, "This is all the Jesus Christ I want."

Oh, my friends, you don't want it to be that way with you. The commandment rings down through the ages, "Thou shalt have no other gods before me." From the Cross Christ says, I am the Way. Come unto Me and you will know the Father and I will guide you through life and take you to heaven at the end of the way.

Sermon 2

NO GRAVEN IMAGES

Thou shalt not make unto thee any graven image, or any likeness of any thing that is in heaven above, or that is in the earth beneath, or that is in the water under the earth. Thou shalt not bow down thyself to them, nor serve them: for I the Lord thy God am a jealous God, visiting the iniquity of the fathers upon the children unto the third and fourth generation of them that hate me; and shewing mercy unto thousands of them that love me, and keep my commandments (Exodus 20:4-6).

The Ten Commandments are divided into two sections. The first four commandments are God-ward, speaking of our duty toward God. The last six are man-ward, speaking of our duty toward man. Jesus summed all of them up on one occasion when someone asked Him which was the greatest commandment. Said He: "Thou shalt love the Lord thy God with all thy heart, and with all thy soul, and with all thy mind, and with all thy strength: . . . Thou shalt love thy neighbor as thyself" (Mark 12:30-31). If we love God with all our heart, soul, mind and strength, we will certainly try to keep the first four commandments, which have to do with our relationship to Him. If we love our neighbor as we do ourselves, we will certainly try to keep the other six commandments, which have to do with our relationship toward other people.

God gave the Ten Commandments as moral laws. Jesus came along and put them on a high spiritual basis. If we follow Him closely these laws shall not trouble our conscience.

The first commandment told us that we were to have no other gods beside Jehovah. The second commandment tells us we are not to make any image and bow down before it. The first commandment tells us who must be worshiped. The second tells us how He must be worshiped. The first commandment forbids all false gods; the second forbids all false worship. Now there is a difference between the first and second commandment. Our Catholic friends don't make this distinction. They throw the second commandment in with the first and pass over it lightly. Why do they do this? Because it conflicts with their world-wide custom of image and statue building. The commandment strictly forbids bowing down before any image. Catholics bow down before statues of Jesus, images of Mary and wooden crosses. It simply means that they are breaking the second commandment.

But they will say, " We do bow down before the image, but we don't worship the image. We are looking beyond the image to Christ." Even so, the Bible says that we are not to bow down to any image or likeness of anything that is in heaven above, the earth beneath, or the water under the earth. Every Roman cathedral and church in the world should have these verses inscribed over its altar. Go to their churches and their hospitals: you will find a crucifix on the wall. Bowing and praying before this image makes worship unreal. Catholics adore a Christ who does not exist — a dead Christ. He is not on the Cross now, but on the Throne. His agonies are over now! He is not the Christ of the bleeding heart; He is our risen, triumphant, reigning Christ. They are praying to a dead Christ.

I. We See Man's Instinct For Worship

Man has certain God-given instincts. His religious instinct is strongest of all. As he battles the forces of nature and humanity, he feels his weakness. As he looks out upon the grandeur of creation, he realizes his littleness. So he reaches out toward an object of worship. His inmost soul cries out for a being greater, stronger, wiser than himself. Every group of people that ever lived has evidenced some sort of religion — either man-made or God-made. Thank God, you and I have the Bible. We know the true God through Jesus Christ the Lord. In recent years ancient cities, buried for thousands of years, have been uncovered. Their civilization may have been crude, but always they left behind them the relics of their religion.

When our forefathers came to these shores they found the original Americans, the Indians. These people had never heard of our God and our Christ, but they worshiped the sun, the moon, the stars, the rivers. They spoke of the Great Spirit. When their braves died their bows and arrows were buried with them. They believed that these braves had gone to the Happy Hunting Ground.

The first settlement in America was not in Jamestown in 1607, but on Roanoke Island off the coast of North Carolina in 1603. The English established a small colony there, but some of the settlers returned to England. When they went back later, this colony had been wiped out by the Indians. I visited this spot several years ago. The state of North Carolina has built there a replica of this lost colony. Right in the center of the village was a small wooden church. I was reminded that men take their religion with them wherever they go.

Plutarch said, "You can find cities without walls, without letters, without money, without houses, without theatres and games, but man has never seen and never will see a city without temples and gods, without prayer, oaths, prophecies and sacrifices." And that is one thing the second commandment tells us — man is going to worship something.

II. Look At What This Commandment Does Not Forbid

It does not forbid all sculpture and painting. God gives certain persons a talent for these things and this talent can be used for the glory of God. The children of Israel murmured against God in the wilderness. Consequently He sent fiery serpents to bite them. Men were soon sick and dying all over the camp. Then God gave the remedy. What was it? He told Moses to make a serpent of brass and to put it upon a pole. Those who looked to this serpent in faith were healed. We see here that God even commanded an image to be made.

Now when the tabernacle was to be built, God told the children of Israel to make many pictures and images. The vail separating the Holy Place from the Most Holy Place was to be adorned with beautiful embroidered figures. Images of cherubims, heavenly creatures, were to be made and placed as guards over the ark of the covenant. They were to make highly decorated golden candlesticks. Even the hems of the priests' garments were to be adorned with bells and pictures of pomegranates.

Later Solomon built the Temple. Look at all the elaborate decorations in it. It was profusely ornamented with images of open flowers, pomegranates, palm trees, oxen, lions and cherubims. And what did God say when the Temple was completed? "I have hallowed this house, which thou hast built, to put my name there forever" (I Kings 9:3). We see here that God was approving a temple of worship adorned with beautiful images. Certainly He is not opposed to our building beautiful houses of worship in His honor today.

So we see that this second commandment does not forbid the making of all images and painting of pictures.

III. WHAT THEN IS EXPRESSLY FORBIDDEN BY THIS COMMANDMENT

Let me put it in the simplest language possible. We are not to make a likeness of anything and bow down before it in worship. We are not to bow before anything for the purpose of religious worship.

Does this mean that we are not to bow down in prayer? No, it does not mean that. When I bow down in prayer, whether it is in the church or in private, I am not bowing before an image, but I am bowing before God. I am not looking at a wooden cross, a statue of Mary, the bleeding side of Jesus, or some saint or angel. I am looking by faith into the face of God. When I pray I don't want any image to hide God's face from me.

The story is told of a wife whose beloved husband has been absent for a year. He is coming home now and she yearns to see him. She stands at the window and waits. She puts his picture on the window sill to help keep his image in her mind. What does the photograph do? It obscures her husband's face from her. She can't see her husband because the picture hides his face. So it is with God. We are not to allow any image to come between us and Him. The best way for us to have communion with God is to close our eyes to everything that can be seen with the natural eye and open the eyes of our spirit toward our Heavenly Father.

Why does man make images and bow down before them? He says, "These images are a great help to me. I know they are not sacred in themselves, but they help me fix my thoughts upon God". A certain man told his pastor that he had been having difficulties in his prayer life. He said that when he prayed it was difficult for him to realize that God was present and listening. The pastor told him to put an empty chair by his bedside, to imagine that God would be there and He would be. The man did this and felt it helped him to pray. He kept up the habit for years. One night he died in his sleep, and in the morning his family found him with one cold hand resting on the chair which he had set aside for his Lord.

In that case the man may have been helped. It may be that when you pray you feel a sense of loneliness and you wonder if God is near. But still remember we are not to bow down before any likeness of God in worship. When you put sin out of your life and let your heart go out in great love and longing toward God, you will soon feel His presence. As the poet has said, He will be "nearer than hands and feet and closer than breathing."

But here is the danger of using an image to assist a person in worship. Here is the reason for this commandment. A man makes an image to assist him in worship and in the end it becomes a snare. The man soon comes to fix his gaze upon the image rather than upon God. He gets absorbed in the picture and loses sight of the Person. He bows before that image one time, a hundred times, a thousand times, and it becomes a habit. He can soon go through all the ritual from memory and never think about God. There is the danger in bowing before images — God is lost sight of.

Today we do not have a true physical picture of Christ. Who knows what He looked like? The Bible doesn't tell us. What color were His eyes? His hair? How tall was He? He didn't leave any keepsakes for His disciples. His clothes were taken by the soldiers. He didn't hand down to us one solitary thing. Maybe He did not leave these things because He knew that we would worship them and not Him. In recent years, we have read stories about the robe which He wore, and the cup from which He drank at the Last Supper.

It has been claimed that certain pieces of the Cross have been found. All of this is pure fiction. He didn't leave one material thing to remind us of Him. He knew if He did men would worship the material and not the Master.

An image of God degrades our conception of Him. It drags God down to our level. Even human beings are sensitive about photographs. No one wants to have a bad picture of himself in circulation. Then how much more must a holy God be filled with a holy wrath when we make an image of Him, because He in reality is so much higher and greater than any image that man can make of Him.

Image worship limits God. It limits Him to one place, and God is omnipresent. An image visualizes God, and He is invisible. God is a spirit, and a spirit cannot be pictured. You cannot take a picture of your soul. So we see that every image of God is false and misleading.

Listen to what God says in Psalm 115:4-8: "Their idols are silver and gold, the work of men's hands. They have mouths, but they speak not: eyes have they, but they see not: They have ears, but they hear not: noses have they, but they smell not: They have hands, but they handle not: feet have they, but they walk not: neither speak they through their throat. They that make them are like unto them; so is everyone that trusteth in them."

A man becomes like that which he worships. The more you bow down before images which are spiritually helpless, the less spiritual power you have. We should be like the Psalmist who cried out, "I will lift up mine eyes unto the hills, from whence cometh my help. My help cometh from the Lord."

Maybe you are saying, "I am innocent — I don't bow down before any image." Yes, but the image may be in your mind. You may be worshiping the god of wealth, the god of popularity, the god of self-indulgence. Men in America worship these things just as surely as men in deepest Africa worship idols.

Many years ago I saw the picture of a young man who wanted to show his contempt for God and show the thing which he really worshiped. He placed his pocketbook, his watch and his jewelry on a shelf and kneeling before them in mockery, he worshiped these things. Oh, my friend, that is a picture of you if you are putting anything else before God.

In McGuffey's Reader is the story of a man who had a subbasement under his regular basement, known only to himself. He kept his silver and his gold in this subbasement. He would come down daily and worship his wealth. He would run his bony fingers through the coins and say, "My beauties, oh, my beauties." One day while he was down there, the wind blew the door of his subbasement shut. It was fastened with a spring lock which could only be turned from the outside. There was no way for the miser to get out. Years later when the house was torn down, the workmen found a skeleton draped over a heap of coins. He had made money his god and his god had destroyed him. Many a man's soul today is destroyed because he bows down and worships some earthly god.

IV. God's Warning About This Commandment

First, God says, "I the Lord thy God am a jealous God." Now we need to understand this word in its right meaning. God's jealousy is not like our jealousy. It is holy and without sin. As used here, it does not mean that God is envious. An envious spirit is always bad. But jealousy as applied to God differs sharply from envy. Here is a man who is insanely jealous. He gets angry when his wife speaks to another man, and wants to kill that man. This is silly and foolish. But he has a right to be jealous if his wife transfers to someone else the affection which is due him. If he loves her, he will be jealous in the right way.

Well, the covenant between God and Israel was a marriage covenant. God was the husband and Israel was the wife. If Israel went out and worshiped someone else, God had a right to be jealous. No sin that a wife can commit against her husband is more degrading than infidelity to the marriage vows. Today the same relationship exists between Christ and the Church. He is the Groom; the Church, made up of Christians, is the Bride. We commit our greatest sin when we give to the world the love which is due to Christ. So let me ask you: Are you bowing down to worldly things, or does Christ have the first love of your heart? He deserves that love, and He has a right to be angry and jealous if you give it to something else.

God then prescribes the punishment for those who violate this commandment, who bow down before other things. "[I will visit] the iniquity of the fathers upon the children unto the third and fourth generation of them that hate me." God doesn't say that He will condemn the children just because their parents are evil. But when the sons follow in the evil footsteps of their fathers, they must suffer for their sin. Surely the children will more likely be guilty of sin if their fathers worship a god other than the God of heaven. Like produces like. A good tree bears good fruit; an evil tree bears evil fruit. If I worship worldly things, it is likely that my children will do the same thing, and they will be punished for it.

God says that the sins of the fathers will be visited upon the children if the children hate God. They are more likely to hate Him if the fathers hated Him before them. So we find here a warning for every parent. Set the right example before your children, live for God, and it is more likely that your children will live for Him. If you put something else in the place of God, you not only hurt yourself, but you hurt your children.

But look at the other side. God says if we love Him and keep His commandments, He will show mercy, not just to the third and fourth generations, but to thousands of generations. "Where sin abounded, grace did much more abound." God's mercy stretches out farther than His wrath. Oh, if I love and serve and worship God, my children and my grandchildren are more likely to do the same thing. Then the blessings will be passed on to future generations. If I love God, He not only blesses me, but He blesses my children.

How then shall we worship God? "In spirit and in truth," Jesus said. We are not to look upon any image, but we are to look up to God in faith. The more we worship Him, the more we become like Him. Our worship is not to be formal. If we go through the same form time after time, the form loses its meaning. Our worship must be spiritual and from the heart. A child learned to say the little prayer, "Now I lay me down to sleep." He kept saying this prayer every night until he was sixty years of age. It was simply a form; it meant nothing to him. Then he found Christ as His Savior and he learned that he really had never prayed before.

Our worship must be spiritual. It must issue from the heart and not from the lips. Worship is simply a child of God having sweet communion with his Heavenly Father. There is private worship, where we go alone with God and pour out our hearts to Him. Then there is public worship, where we come together to sing, to pray, to give, to listen to the Gospel, and to partake of the Lord's Supper. Every Christian should practice both private and public worship.

Let me close this message with two contrasting pictures. The captain of a whaling vessel attended a church in New England. After the service someone asked him what impression the service made upon him. He replied, "No impression was made. As the congregation sang and as the pastor preached I was thinking about where I could find my next whale. There is no room in my heart for anything but whales." An old preacher lay dying. His house was near the church where he had ministered and worshiped. On Sunday morning as the church bells rang, he raised his head and whispered, "I want . . . I want." They leaned closer to hear what he was saying and the dear old man of God whispered, "I want to worship God."

Listen, my friends, I want to draw as close to Christ as I can while I make my way through this world. And some day, when life's little day is done, I want to meet Him in heaven, and with nothing between us, I want to fall down before Him and worship Him forever and ever.

Sermon 3

DO NOT TAKE GOD'S NAME IN VAIN

Thou shalt not take the name of the Lord thy God in vain; for the Lord will not hold him guiltless that taketh his name in vain (Exodus 20:7).

The first commandment told us that we are to worship God and Him only. The second commandment told us not to bow down before any image, but to worship Him in spirit and in truth. The third commandment tells us that we are to reverence Him: we are never to use His holy name in the wrong way. "Well, preacher," you say, "you are going to talk to us about profanity, aren't you?" Yes, but there is much more involved in this commandment. It forbids profanity, but it forbids much more.

Listen to this commandment: "Thou shalt not take the name of the Lord thy God in vain; for the Lord will not hold him guiltless that taketh His name in vain." What is the most important thought in this commandment? Here it is: "The name of the Lord."

I. The Name of the Lord

There is something unique and different about God's name. Today names don't always mean very much. A boy may be named George Washington and grow up to be the biggest liar in the country. A boy may be named "Honest Abe" after

Abraham Lincoln and become the biggest crook in the community. A boy may be named Truett or Spurgeon after one of the great preachers, and become a drunkard and a wastrel. But in Bible times names held meaning indicative of character. Abraham meant "Father of the Faithful"; Jacob, "Supplanter"; Israel, "Prince with God"; John, "Jehovah's gift"; and Peter, "a rock."

Now God's name means something. It is different from all others. It is grander and higher and more significant than all other names. Modern thinkers call Him "The Great Unknown," or "The Absolute," or "The Great First Cause." But in the Bible He gives us the meanings of His names. Jehovah meant "the Self-existent and Unchangeable One." Elohim meant "the One filled with Majesty — the One to be Feared." This is the name used in the first sentence of the Bible where we are told that God created the heavens and the earth. El meant "the Strong and Powerful One"; Adonai, "Lord or Ruler"; Eljon, "the Exalted One"; and El-Shaddai, "the All High."

So we see that all God is, does, and says is included in His name. The commandment does not simply forbid the vain use of God's name, but all irreverence to God Himself. God is holy; man is human. God is perfect; man is sinful. God is high above all; men are lowly sinners. Man owes Him reverence, awe, fear, and respect. When man does not show proper reverence for God he is breaking this commandment.

God's name is holy, even as He is holy. There is something personal and individual about a name. A man doesn't like to see his name misspelled or hear it mispronounced. If that is true of us, how much more is it true of God. His name reveals Himself and is not to be separated from Him. When we show disrespect for His name, we show disrespect for God. We honor the names of great men. In government we honor Washington, Jefferson and Lincoln. In religion we honor Luther, Calvin and Spurgeon. How much more, then, should we honor the name of God! In honoring His name we honor Him.

II. THE WRONG USE OF GOD'S NAME

1. *The wrong use in profanity.* It shouldn't be necessary to speak to a Christian congregation about profanity, but it is one of the most common sins of the day. I fear that many Christians are guilty of this sin. This is a cursing age. Men curse, women curse, children curse. They curse on the streets, on the job, in the home, at parties, everywhere. This is a sad commentary on our social life.

What earthly good does profanity do? A man has a flat tire and he curses the tire. But that doesn't put air into the tire. A man stumbles upon a chair in the dark and he curses the chair, but that doesn't heal the bruise. A man curses because he loses a game he is playing, but his cursing doesn't win the game. There is absolutely no reward in profanity. Every other sin pays off, but not profanity. If you steal or drink or commit adultery there is some satisfaction in it. It pays off somewhere along the line, but there is no pay-off when you use profanity.

One day I approached a man I know who was cursing a blue streak. When he turned around and saw me, he said, "Excuse, me preacher, I didn't know you were present." I told him that I was not the one to whom he should apologize. He had taken the Lord's name in vain, and he should apologize to the Lord. If it is wrong to curse when the preacher hears you, it is wrong to curse any time. Remember that God hears you, wherever you are and whatever you say. Your speech is an index to your character. I listen to a man speak and I know what he is. If he speaks German, he is likely to be a German. If he speaks French, he is likely to be a Frenchman. If he speaks in profanity, I know that his heart is sinful. Jesus said, "Out of the abundance of the heart the mouth speaketh." Pure water comes out of a pure well: impure water out of a polluted well. It is the same with the heart.

Sam Jones, a great evangelist of another day, said, "When I hear a man cursing I hold to my pocketbook. If he will break one of God's laws, he is likely to break another. If he will curse, he may steal." Every cursing man is not a dishonest man, but surely he stands guilty before God.

It may surprise you to know that profanity is much more common in so-called Christian America than in the heathen countries. Heathens have greater reverence for their false gods than we do for our Heavenly Father. A missionary was returning from India. He had his little son on the ship with him. This little boy had never been to America. One day an American on deck was indulging in profuse profanity. The missionary went to him and said, "Sir, my little boy was born and brought up in a heathen land, in a land of idolatry, but in all his life he has never heard a man blaspheme his Maker until now." Isn't that a sad commentary? We know God, He has richly blessed us, and yet we continue to take His name in vain.

When you curse you offer a profane and wicked prayer. You ask God to condemn someone in order to satisfy your passion for revenge. Jesus said, "Thou shalt love thy neighbour as thyself." He also said, "And as ye would that men should do to you, do ye also to them." Instead of doing that, you ask God to damn someone. Don't you see how awful your sin is?

Then sometimes you say to a man, "Go to hell." Now God has prepared hell for the Devil and his angels. It is a terrible place. Jesus said that men live on there forever in suffering and shame. This is a fact too solemn to be trifled with in conversation. Men are going to hell, but it is not your place to condemn them.

Profanity not only corrupts you, but it corrupts others. Your child hears your profanity and takes it up. This soon leads to something much worse. You do not sin alone — you hurt someone else when you use profanity. Yet some intelligent men and women swear as if they had gone to school in hell and had the Devil for their teacher. It is not a sign of intelligence and maturity to be able to curse. It often shows the lack of a good vocabulary. If you take a few curse words away from some persons, they are not able to carry on a conversation.

George Washington said, "The foolish and wicked practice of profane cursing and swearing is a vice so mean and so low that every person of sense and character detests and despises it."

Now let me tell you, young people, that being able to curse is not the mark of a man. You live in a Christian home and your parents and the influence of your church keep your speech clean while you are growing up, but when you go out into the world you will find an atmosphere full of profanity. It will grieve you to hear the name of the Lord taken in vain. But after a time the shock wears away and you get used to it. One day you begin to swear and it soon becomes a habit. I tell you that this is a sin in the sight of God. It doesn't help your standing with good people; it doesn't gain anything for you, it cheapens you in every way.

Let me tell you my experience. I learned some wicked words when I was a teen-age boy. One day I became angry in front of a certain man and spat out a stream of profanity. He was a good man and he really gave me a "dressing down."

I went out from his presence ashamed and humiliated. The years have gone by, but I have never forgotten the lesson I learned that day. But that is not the thing that cured me. Several years later I found Jesus Christ as my Savior. When He came into my heart, the profanity had to go. There was no place there for it. I became a new man in Christ Jesus and the old things of profanity passed away.

2. *Then there is the wrong use of God's name in hypocrisy.* When a man says, "Lord, Lord," and lives a sinful life, he is guilty of breaking this commandment. Profanity in church is worse than profanity on the street. When our prayers are denied by our lives, when our praise is counteracted by our sins, then we have taken God's name in vain. When a man comes to church and confesses Christ with his lips, but denies Him with his life, he has a far worse influence than the man who makes no profession of religion at all. Before I entered the ministry, I was a member of a church in Atlanta. A certain deacon in that church had a very pious attitude. He condemned all sin and criticized all worldliness. When the pastor called upon him for prayer, he could offer a very pious prayer and you would almost think that he was talking to God face to face. Yet, all the time this man was stealing nearly a million dollars of sacred mission money from our Home Mission Board. He was guilty of breaking this commandment in hypocrisy.

Once upon a time a donkey suddenly got rich. He thought he was too good to associate with other donkeys, so he decided to become a horse. He went to the hair-dresser, had his ears trimmed and pinned down, and then went out into the high society of horses. Everything went along all right until he was asked to sing. The minute he opened his mouth, they knew what he was — a hypocrite. So it is that men today go among

the people of God and profess to be great Christians, but
their hearts are black with sin, for they don't know Jesus
Christ. They are breaking this commandment in hypocrisy.

Sacred music is a wonderful thing and lifts us up toward
God. But many people stand behind the songbook and sing a
lie. They never carry into practice what they sing with their
lips. They sing, "My Jesus, I love Thee, I know Thou art
mine, for Thee all the follies of sin I resign." Right then
they know that they are not willing to give up anything for
Christ. They sing, "Take my silver and my gold," but they
are not willing to part with one penny. They sing, "Have
thine own way," and they go their way. They sing, "I sur-
render all," when in truth they have given nothing for Christ.
It is hypocrisy to sing and talk of the love of God and to
live for the Devil. This is taking the name of the Lord in
vain.

3. *Then there is the wrong use of God's name in empty
vows.* Any man who makes a pledge to the Lord and breaks
that pledge has taken his name in vain. Here is a man who
is sick or in great trouble. He knows that he needs the Lord
at this time, and he calls upon Him, making a vow that he will
live for God the rest of his days. When his trouble is over,
he promptly forgets God, goes his own way and thus he
breaks this commandment.

In 1923 a great earthquake struck Japan. Thousands of
people lost their lives and thousands more were left homeless.
America raised millions of dollars and sent this money over
to help the Japanese. The Japanese were very grateful and
said, "Japan will never forget." A few years ago, when I was
in Hawaii, I went to Pearl Harbor. There I could see part
of the warship *Arizona* jutting up out of the water. The
bodies of 1,400 American boys are sealed in that ship. It
is their tomb. For on December 7, 1941, Japan did forget all

that America had done for her. Japan bombed Pearl Harbor and plunged us into a bloody war. But this is not as bad as a man who has been greatly blessed of God, who says, "I will never forget," and who soon leaves God entirely out of his life.

An old man was walking through a forest in Canada. He heard a man speaking, and coming to an open place, he found giving an infidel lecture — he was denying the existence of God. The old man waited patiently until the young man had finished and then he mounted the stump. "Ladies and gentlemen," he said, "I will not argue with this young man, but I will tell you something that happened two days ago. I was walking by the Niagara River when I heard a cry for help. I saw a young man caught in the current and being carried toward the falls. He was calling upon God and promising to live for God if He would save him. I went to his rescue — I risked my own life to save his life. This young man who called upon God two days ago is the same young man who has just stood before you and told you that there is no God." He had made an empty vow; he had broken this commandment.

I know many people who have pledged to tithe. But when the time came for them to pay their vow, they used the money for something else and broke their pledge to God. They didn't even give God a chance to bless them.

> When thou shalt vow a vow unto the Lord thy God, thou shalt not slack to pay it: for the Lord thy God will surely require it of thee; and it would be sin in thee (Deut. 23:21).
> When thou vowest a vow unto God, defer not to pay it; for he hath no pleasure in fools: pay that which thou hast vowed (Eccl. 5:4).

So we see that we can break the third commandment in profanity, in hypocrisy, and in making empty vows.

III. The Right Use Of God's Name

1. *We can use His name in profession.* "Whosoever therefore shall confess me before men, him will I confess also before my Father which is in heaven." We do the right thing when we walk down the aisle and confess Him before all the world as our Lord and Savior.

2. *We can use His name in prayer.* It is certainly right for us to come reverently and humbly before God and to call upon His name in earnest prayer.

3. *We can use His name in praise.* When we think of all of His blessings and when we stand to testify, we can use His name in praise of His goodness. We can sing His praises always. We can use His name in real worship.

4. *We can use His name in taking legal oaths.* Such oaths are not forbidden; they are often used in the Bible. An oath is used to satisfy others as to our sincerity and truthfulness. A man stands before a court. With one hand on the Bible and the other hand lifted toward heaven, he promises to tell "the truth, the whole truth, and nothing but the truth, so help me, God." When a man breaks this oath, the court calls it perjury. The Bible calls it the taking of the name of the Lord in vain. It is the breaking of the third commandment. Of course, it is a sin to invoke God to witness to a lie.

IV. The Penalty For Breaking This Commandment

Here it is: The Lord will not hold him guiltless. If you are guilty, God will punish you. "But," you say, "my profanity is just a habit—I don't mean any harm." God says, "I will not hold you guiltless."

The church at Jerusalem was flourishing. Spirit was running high. The Christians were so anxious to see others saved that they sold their property and brought their money to the church to be used in the work of soul winning. In the group was a couple named Ananias and Sapphira. They decided to sell their land, bring part of the money to the church, and keep the balance for themselves. The next day we see Ananias bringing a sum of money to the church. Peter asked him whether he sold the land for so much: Ananias replied that he did. Peter blazed out at him, "Why hath Satan filled thine heart to lie? . . . thou hast not lied unto men, but unto God." Ananias fell dead right there, and the young men took him out and buried him. Three hours later his wife came in, not knowing what had happened. Peter asked her: "Tell me whether ye sold the land for so much:" She lied just as Ananias had done. Immediately she fell dead at Peter's feet and was taken out and buried by the side of her husband. You say that it is not a very serious thing to take the Lord's name in vain as did Ananias and Sapphira. But as you watch these young men burying Ananias and Sapphira, you should realize that it is a serious thing to take the Lord's name in vain. God will not hold you guiltless.

Ah, but in spite of our sin, we have the assurance that God loves us and will forgive us if we repent of our sins. He says, "Though your sins be as scarlet, they shall be as white as snow." Peter swore one day, saying that he didn't know Jesus. In a few minutes Jesus came by and looked at him with love, mercy and forgiveness. Peter went out and wept bitterly. We never hear of him taking the Lord's name in vain again. And when we repent as he did, the same mercy and forgiveness shall be ours.

Sam Hadley for many years was head of the Water Street Mission in New York. He walked with a limp. He had never been in the army, but before his conversion he said that he limped because of wounds received in battle. The day after his conversion, when a man asked him why he limped, he forgot himself and lied about his army service. Suddenly he real-ized that he had lied, and he wanted to correct the lie. But the man was gone, so he caught a street car, went down to the man's office and confessed that he had lied to him a few minutes before. That is what Christ can do for you. He can make you over inside. The only way to keep any of these commandments is to turn your life over to Jesus Christ.

While Dwight L. Moody was holding a meeting in Chicago a certain man requested prayer for himself. After the meeting, Mr. Moody found the man under deep conviction, but he did not have the courage to come out for Christ. He was afraid of what his friends might say. Sometime later this man was sick and sent for Mr. Moody. Mr. Moody talked and prayed with him. The man promised that he would give his heart to Christ when he was well again. Soon the man was up and about and Mr. Moody said, "You certainly will take a stand now for Christ." The man replied, "I promised God I would do this when I was on my sickbed, but I want to wait a while. I am going to buy a farm and settle down and then I will become a Christian." Mr. Moody insisted that the man settle the matter right then. But the man replied, "No, Mr. Moody, I will wait until spring. You have done your duty, and if I die without Christ, it will not be your fault." One week later the man's wife sent for Mr. Moody, because the man was sick again. Mr. Moody tried to talk with him and the man said, "It is no use, it's too late now. I made my promise to Christ and I broke it." Mr. Moody said, "But God is merciful." And the man whispered, "The harvest is passed, the summer is ended and I am not saved." Soon he had gone into eternity without God and without hope.

Am I talking to one who has been promising God that he would give his heart to Christ and join the church and live for Him? Oh, my friend, don't put off this matter! You have taken the name of the Lord in vain and God will not hold you guiltless. Come to Jesus now.

Sermon 4

NO DESECRATION OF THE LORD'S DAY

> Remember the sabbath day, to keep it holy. Six days shalt thou labour, and do all thy work: but the seventh day is the sabbath of the Lord thy God: in it thou shalt not do any work, thou, nor thy son, nor thy daughter, nor thy manservant, nor thy maidservant, nor thy cattle, nor thy stranger that is within thy gates: for in six days the Lord made heaven and earth, the sea, and all that in them is, and rested the seventh day: wherefore the Lord blessed the sabbath day, and hallowed it (Exodus 20:8-11).

The first commandment told us to worship God and none other. The second told us to worship Him directly and to have no idols. The third told us to worship Him sincerely and not falsely. The fourth tells us of a special time set aside for worship. "But," you will say, "I thought that a Christian could worship at any time." That is true, and we ought to worship morning, noon and night. But God in His infinite wisdom knew that we would need one special time, one special day to call our attention away from earth to heaven, from man to God. So He set aside one day out of seven as a special day of worship.

I. The Day Set Aside

God, not man set aside one day of the week for rest and worship. He did this long before He gave the Ten Commandments. In Genesis 2 we read, "And on the seventh day

47

God ended his work which he had made; and he rested on the seventh day from all his work which he had made. And God blessed the seventh day, and sanctified it: because that in it he had rested from all his work which God created and made."

The story of creation is a dramatic one. God began His work by creating light and dividing it from the darkness. This He did on the first day of creation. Then He worked the second day, the third, the fourth, the fifth. Then on the sixth day He made man and put him in the Garden of Eden. God looked upon all that He had done and saw that it was good, so He rested from His labors of creation. Does this mean that God was tired, exhausted, and needed physical rest? No, in the Book of Isaiah we read that God is never weary. He didn't need to lie down and rest after He created the world. It simply means that the work of creation had ceased, even though His other work went on. Here is an artist who paints his masterpiece and then steps back and looks with pleasure upon his work. So God, having finished the work of creation, steps back and pauses to take divine pleasure in the work He had done.

Now, the word "Sabbath" doesn't mean a particular day. It simply means a period of rest — for God it was the seventh day. So we see, then, that the Sabbath was not invented in Moses' day, but that it goes back to the creation. When you trace the history of all the ancient peoples of the world — the Israelites, the Assyrians, the Egyptians, the Arabians, the Persians — you find that they always made use of a week consisting of seven days. How can you account for this uniformity? I am sure that God was behind it all. And the Sabbath was observed on the seventh day of the week from the time that God created the world.

Here is an illustration. The children of Israel were on their forty-year journey from Egypt to the Promised Land. They had to eat, so God sent manna from heaven. Each day the people gathered as much as they needed (if they gathered more than they needed, the manna would spoil). But on the sixth day Moses told the people to gather twice as much as they needed, so that they would have enough for the Sabbath day — and it would not spoil. Some persons went out on the Sabbath day to gather manna and found none. God, therefore, was keeping the Sabbath day long before He gave the Ten Commandments, and He expected His people to keep it. God not only set aside the day, but He blessed and hallowed it. The Sabbath day stands out by itself; it is not like any other day. God has made of it a special day, and when we treat it like any other day we are sinning against God.

God set the example for us by resting on the Sabbath day. Example teaches more than precept, so God points to Himself as the highest example. We must keep one day holy, because God did. Paul exhorts Christians to be imitators of God. God is the model after which we are to pattern our lives. He has a right to demand that we keep one day for Him. He gave us our existence; He provides for us daily. He gives us six days for ourselves; He is not being unreasonable in claiming one day for Himself. If we profane His day, we are robbing God. We commit a crime against heaven when we take something which belongs to God and use it for ourselves. We have no right to steal something which belongs to anyone, much less God.

II. THE PURPOSE OF THE SABBATH DAY

We have already seen that when God set aside the Sabbath day He ceased from His labors and delighted in His work. He has the same purpose for man. He gives him a day to rest from his own work and to delight himself in the things of God. Jesus said, "The sabbath was made for man, and not man for the sabbath." He meant that God set aside the day to benefit man. God is always thinking of man. He is always doing something for him. The Sabbath is one of God's best gifts to man.

After a man works six days he needs a day of rest for the preservation of health and strength. A man's body needs restoration. It has been proved by actual test that a man can do more work by working six days a week and resting one than by working seven days a week without any rest. Talmadge said, "Our bodies are seven-day clocks and need to be wound up. If they are not wound up, they run down into the grave. No man can continually break the Sabbath and keep his physical and mental health."

During the French Revolution, when atheism was at its height, the French people decided to abolish the Lord's Day. Instead of having one day's rest out of seven, they had one out of ten. But it didn't work, because it was not according to God's plan.

This commandment not only says that a man needs a day of rest; it also provides for the relief of his working animals. The ox and the ass also were to have a day off. A man tells of seeing two groups of donkeys at a mountain resort. They were used to carry sight-seers to a top of a lofty mountain. One group of animals looked well-kept, the other lean and weary. Why the difference? One man sent his donkeys up the mountain seven days a week; the other refused to work his more than six days each week. Even a donkey knows that one day in seven should be used as a day of rest.

In the olden days the slaves of the South sang this song, "Every day will be Sunday bye and bye." Sunday was a day when the burdens were lifted and they could rest. They looked forward to the time in heaven when every day would be like Sunday.

For twenty-one years Ashley's Restaurant in El Paso was kept open every Sunday. Then on one wonderful Sunday morning, Mr. Ashley walked down the aisle of our church and gave his heart to Christ. Immediately he closed the restaurant on Sunday, urged his employees to go to church and became a faithful Christian and church member himself. Since that time God has wondrously blessed him in every way.

Several years ago a man opened a bakery across the street from our church. He put a sign in the window which said, "Open every Sunday." I went over to see him and talked the matter over with him. I told him that I believed God would bless his business if he would close up on Sunday. He agreed to do this and God did bless his business beyond all of his expectations. He often thanked me for talking to him as I did.

As we think of a man resting one day a week, we must not forget the other part of the commandment, "six days shalt thou labor." It is God's plan for every man to be a worker. He has no patience with a lazy idler. When He put Adam and Eve in the Garden of Eden, He commissioned them to dress and keep the garden. When sin came, their work became burdensome and the curse of work now is that it is done in the sweat of the face. When we get to heaven, we shall still be active. But the sting will be taken out of our labors and all the work that we do will be refreshing and invigorating.

The Sabbath day was not only a day of rest, but a day of worship. This is a different kind of rest. Cessation from work rests the body, while worship rests and invigorates the soul. Today a man spends six days looking after the material things of life. He needs one day to look after the spiritual side. "Man shall not live by bread alone." Yes, God gives us one day when we should cease from our labors. But He didn't intend for us to spend that day in bed! He meant for us to give some time and thought to Him and His work and His church.

Now the Pharisees of Jesus' time went to the extreme. They turned a day of gladness into a day of gloom. They discovered 1,500 ways in which a man could break the Sabbath. He could not kindle a fire on the Sabbath, no matter how cold he was. If a man's ox fell into the ditch, he could pull him out, but if a man fell into the ditch, he had to stay there. If a man was bitten by a flea he had to permit the flea to keep on biting. If he tried to catch the flea he would be guilty of the sin of hunting on the Sabbath.

When the Puritans came to America they held the same idea. They thought this was pure religion. A certain sea captain who lived in Massachuestts had been absent from home for two years. He returned home on Sunday and his wife met him at the gate and he kissed her. This was not lawful, so the puritans put him in the stocks for desecrating the Sabbath.

I don't think it is God's plan to make Sunday a miserable day for us. It is not a good idea to make children sit quietly in a corner and read the Bible all of Sunday afternoon. In that way they are made to hate Sunday and all that it stands for.

Man has a direct relationship to God. God created him and redeems him when he comes to Christ. There must be a time when that relationship is considered, so God has set aside a day for it. If a man has no Sabbath, he has no relationship to God. If a man never gets more than six days away from God, it is not hard to call him back to God. But it is extremely difficult to bring a man back to God who has had no relationship with Him for fifteen or twenty years. Each

Sunday brings a foretaste of heaven. Hell is separation from God. The man who has no Sabbath has no fellowship with God. He is now living more in hell than in heaven.

Gladstone, the grand old man of England, lived to be eighty-nine years of age. He was strong and vigorous even in his later years. When someone asked him the secret of his vigor, he told a little story. He said that there was a road in England on which more horses died than any other road. When asked the reason for this, he said that the road was perfectly level and the horses which traveled this road used only one set of muscles and consequently their stamina was lowered. It is the same way with man. If a man always goes along on the dead level of the world, if he never has the lift of the Lord's Day, it affects his whole life and he becomes a weaker and sorrier person.

A man was passing a coal mine in Pennsylvania one Sunday. Seeing a number of mules in the field he asked a boy what the mules were used for. The boy replied, "These mules work in the mine all the week. If they were not brought up on Sunday they would go blind." My friends, the same thing is true of us. If we treat Sunday like any other day, if we don't seek some spiritual light, our spiritual eyes become blinded.

The Sabbath day is an emblem of eternal rest. When the week's work is over we rest from our labors and we find our way to God's House. There we enjoy fellowship with Him and with the children of God. So, when life's work is over, we shall rest from our labors in the Father's House above. We shall glory forever in His redemptive work and enjoy sweet and everlasting fellowship with God and His family.

III. The Day Changed

We have been talking about the Sabbath, which is an Old Testament term. We come now to think of its successor, which in the New Testament is called "the Lord's Day." The early Christians observed the first day of the week because of the resurrection of Christ. Jesus did not change the Sabbath, but He did change the day. In the Old Testament economy the last day of the week was set aside to commemorate the finished work of creation. Now the first day of the week is set aside to commemorate the finished work of redemption. The redemption of the souls of men is more important than the creation of a world.

Jesus went down to the tomb and stayed there through the Jewish Sabbath. There He grappled with death and defeated the monster. On the first day of the week, He rose triumphant from the dead. Now that day is forever emblazoned on the scrolls of history as Christ's royal, triumphant day. Christ buried the institutions, the offerings and the sacrifices of the Old Testament in that tomb. Now we live in a new age, an age of new institutions and offerings. And He has given us a new day — the Lord's Day. Saturday is the Sabbath of nature; Sunday is the day of grace. Saturday is the Sabbath of the rejected, crucified, entombed Christ; Sunday is the day of the risen, exalted, triumphant Christ! Saturday is the Creator's day; Sunday is the Redeemer's day!

New Testament history proves that the first day of the week is the Lord's Day. (1) Five times did Jesus appear — each time on the first day of the week. (2) The Holy Spirit descended when the believers were meeting on the first day of the week. (3) The Lord's Supper was always celebrated on the first day of the week. (4) Paul said that we were to make our offerings on the first day of the week. (5) John, on the Isle of Patmos, said that he was "in the spirit on the Lord's Day." The first day of the week, the Lord's Day, was universally observed by the Christians of the first century.

The first day of the week has been observed by the Christian Church for two thousand years. On Sunday millions of people have heard the Gospel in their churches and have been saved. On Sunday millions of weary hearts have found their way to God's House and there they have found peace and rest. On Sunday millions of broken-hearted people have come to church and found comfort. Oh, what would we do without Sunday, the Lord's Day! Nowhere in the New Testament are we taught that the Lord's Day is the seventh day. Those who insist on keeping the seventh day forget that Christ is risen. They are living on the wrong side of Calvary.

Jesus died on the eve of the Jewish Sabbath. The Old Sabbath died with Him. He was in the grave during the Jewish Sabbath. The old Sabbath was buried with Him. He arose right after the Jewish Sabbath. There is a new day for us because of His resurrection.

IV. The Desecration Of The Day

Jesus meant for His day to be different from others. It is true that today men make it different, but in the wrong way. For many people Sunday is the most hectic day of the week. It is the day when some of our biggest athletic contests are attended by the biggest crowds. It is the day when some of our church people give their most elaborate parties. It is the day of the biggest picnics, the day when the largest crowds flock to the theaters. It is the day when the roads are most congested with traffic, when most wrecks occur, and when most people are injured or killed.

The majority of people sacrifice Sunday upon the altar of the twin gods, profit and pleasure. One group is trying to make profit out of the day; the other group is seeking worldly pleasure. Radio and television have just about ruined many of our Sunday evening services. Why? Because so many people put these things above Christ. They would rather sit at home and watch the vaudeville actors of America than to come to church, where they can worship God and witness to the unsaved. Even the large Sunday paper comes between many people and the Lord.

Every baseball fan knows that for years Philadelphia had a baseball team called the Athletics. For years Sunday baseball was not allowed in Philadelphia. But the owner of the Athletics, Connie Mack, went before the state legislature and told them that if they could not have Sunday baseball his team would be ruined financially. Huge sums of money were spent in lobbying and finally in 1933 Sunday baseball won out by two votes. What has happened since that time? Before that time the Athletics had one of the strongest teams in the major leagues. They won several American League pennants and several world championships. In 1933 Sunday baseball was started in Philadelphia. The Athletics have not won a single pennant since that time. In 1954 a group of business men tried to save the team and keep it in Philadelphia. They were not able to do so; therefore the team was moved to Kansas City. The money interests fought against God and won a temporary victory. But God had the last word and He won the final victory.

A group of young people wrote to Dr. Robert G. Lee, "We are all active in a Baptist church. We play softball on Sunday afternoon and quit in time to go to Training Union. Is this wrong?" Of course, Dr. Lee told them that it was wrong. Even if you do go to church Sunday morning and Sunday night, if you attend a picture show or a ball game, or play golf on Sunday afternoon, you haven't kept the day holy. God said that the entire day was to be kept holy, not just the part which is used for church services.

When you forget the Lord's Day you are on the way to

forgetting God. The man who treats Sunday as any other day never has any time for church or spiritual things. God means nothing to him. He will go on the merry way of the world, and at the end of the way the God whom he has forgotten and the Christ whom he has rejected will condemn him to an eternity in hell. He will have time to think then, but it will be too late.

An English gentleman was inspecting a house in New Castle with intentions of buying it. The owner took him to an upper window and said, "On Sunday you can see Durham Cathedral from here." "How is that?" asked the man. And the owner replied, "On Sunday there is no smoke from the chimneys to obstruct the view." Oh, I tell you that we need a day when the smoke is cleared away from our eyes and when we look up to see God and get new strength for life.

V. The Duties Of The Day

1. *We are to rest.* God says, "Be still and know that I am God." We need a little time to turn aside from the restless fever of life and to think of Him. Sunday should be set aside to minister to the physical, spiritual and mental needs of man.

2. *We are to worship.* Primarily, this means gathering in God's house with God's people for this purpose. "Not forsaking the assembling of ourselves together, as the manner of some is; but exhorting one another: and so much the more, as ye see the day approaching" (Heb. 10:25).

God took pleasure in His works on the Sabbath day. Our Sundays are to be used to take delight, also, in the things of God. The man who says that he can be as good a Christian by staying away from church as by attending, is saying that God made a mistake in setting aside the day, and that Christ made a mistake in placing the church on the earth. We are weak creatures and we need the external supports which we find in hearing the Gospel, in having fellowship with the saints and in service in the Lord's House.

The man who lets Sunday go by without thinking of the goodness of God and His salvation in Christ, who absolutely forgets His death, His burial, His resurrection, and His coming again, is the basest ingrate in the world. He is a man who doesn't deserve the consideration of a loving God, and who rightfully will end up in an eternal hell.

Soren Kierkegaard gives us this parable of the end of time. A theater was crowded with patrons, when a fire broke out in the rear of the building. The manager did not want a panic, so he sent a popular actor out upon the stage to make an announcement about the fire. This actor gave the message about the fire and told the people to leave in a quiet and orderly fashion. But they thought he was just acting, and they began to applaud him. He repeated his message and they cried out with delight at the artistry of his make-believe. Once more he made an impassioned plea. The people applauded him again, but sat where they were. Then the walls collapsed and the crowd was destroyed. In like manner, God's voice is the voice of thunder telling us of the coming judgment. He warns us to flee the wrath to come. Oh, do not merely applaud God, but listen to Him! Sunday is your day to hear Him. Find your way to His House, listen to His Gospel, obey His voice and walk in His ways.

Sir Winston Churchill was visiting the White House on June 27, 1954. President Eisenhower invited him to go to church with him, but he stated that he had rather rest in his air-conditioned suite in the White House. In December, 1953, when they were attending the Bermuda Conference, President Eisenhower invited him to go to church and Mr.

Churchill smilingly replied, as he declined the invitation, "I will meet my Maker soon enough." Poor Mr. Churchill. He is wise in so many of the things of this world and so foolish about the things of God. The greatest reason in the world that we should go to church is to meet God now and to worship Him now.

3. *Sunday is also to be used for service.* Jesus healed people on the Sabbath, thus setting the example for us. We can serve the Lord in His church and perform acts of mercy toward others on the Lord's Day. Longfellow said, "Sunday is the golden clasp that binds together the volume of the week." Let me tell you that life is meaningless unless you set aside a special day for God.

One night a man arose in Tremont Temple in Boston and said, "Nearly twenty years ago I brought a poor, drunken fellow into this church one night. He listened to the sermon and was convicted of his sin. He was saved that night. I don't know where that man is now, but I thank God for that Sunday night and that salvation." On the other side of the church a man arose and said, "I am your man; you brought me here that Sunday night. I found Christ that night and He has been my Savior ever since. I thank God for that Sunday."

Let us also thank God for Sunday — every Sunday — and let us use every Sunday in the right way.

Sermon 5

HONOR THY FATHER AND THY MOTHER

Honour thy father and thy mother: that thy days may be
long upon the land which the Lord thy God giveth thee
(Exodus 20:12).

The relationships of a man are in two directions. He owes
an obligation to God and an obligation to man. He has both
a vertical and a horizontal relationship. While we would all
admit that our obligations to God are the more important,
we must also realize that a man has not done his full duty
until he has discharged his obligations to both God and man.

Now this truth forever holds. If we are right in our relationships to God, we shall also adjust our lives so as to fulfill
all our obligations to mankind. The first four commandments
have to do with our relationship to God. The fifth commandment marks the turning point, for the last six commandments
speak of our relationship to others. If we keep the first four
commandments truly, sincerely, earnestly, it will not be hard
to keep the last six. If your heart is right toward God, you will
treat your mother and father rightly, you will not kill, you
will not commit adultery, you will not steal, you will not
bear false witness, you will not covet. These last six commandments are called the marble pillars which hold up the
social order in the world.

Let me tell you that the ten commandments are not just
laws — they are love. The first four tell us to love God above

all; the final six tell us to love other people as much as we love ourselves. The fifth commandment tells us to love and honor our parents. Among all the people of the world, they are the first ones whom we meet. So God put the commandment in the right place. Before we can love and respect strangers, we must learn to love and respect our parents, the first people we meet when we come into the world.

I. The Commandment

"Honor thy father and thy mother." God first tells us of our duties toward Him; then He begins with the family. He doesn't tell us how soldiers should fight, or how merchants should conduct their business, or how teachers should teach, or preachers preach. But He tells us how sons and daughters should treat their mothers and fathers. The family is a divine institution. God established it. It is the foundation of all human society. When the home decays, the church decays and the state decays. And the home decays when we don't have the right relationship between the children and their parents.

1. *We honor our parents by giving them the proper respect and reverence.* We are never to call them "the old man" or "the old lady." In heathenism we find that the children have the greatest respect for their parents. Americans have gone too far the other way and this is a dangerous trend. We owe an obligation to our parents which we will never be able to pay, even if we devoted our entire lives to making them happy.

In a magazine article a man tells about conversing on a train with a young Japanese boy who had not been in America very long. An American mother and her twelve-year-old son sat opposite them. The mother said, "Son, please go and get me a drink of water." The boy replied, "I won't do it." The man said that the Japanese boy jumped as if a bomb had exploded under him. He told the man that he had never seen nor heard anything like that in Japan. Fifty years ago the average American child wouldn't have dared to raise his voice against his parents. Now it is common.

Think of what we owe our parents. We are obligated to them for life itself. They gave us life, they brought us into the world, their very blood flows in our veins. Then they gave us love. Unless your parents are ridiculously abnormal, they have loved you every day that you have lived. Now, because God loved us and gave His Son to die for us, He expects and demands our gratitude. Nothing in the world is so like God's love as the love of a good mother and father. Therefore, this love places us under greatest obligation to them. Shakespeare says, "How sharper than a serpent's tooth it is to have a thankless child."

Then think of the sacrifices which our parents made for us. Your father may be a plain man, your mother may not be too attractive, but they made many sacrifices to bring you to the position which you occupy today. My father was a poor, hard-working man, with not many things of this earth to enjoy. But he did the best he could for his children. He died one June day as I sat by his bedside and held his hand. A thousand times since then I have wished that I had done more and said more to show my appreciation for all that he tried to do for me. Oh, we never know when they are going to leave us, so we ought to say and do things now to show our appreciation for their love and sacrifice!

Look how strong the Bible is on this matter of honoring parents.

> And he that smiteth his father, or his mother, shall be surely put to death (Exodus 21:15).
> And he that curseth his father, or his mother, shall surely be put to death (Exodus 21:17).

God says here that if you curse or strike one of your parents, you deserve to be put to death. So we see that this command to honor them is the foundation of Christian duty, decency and morality.

David had a son named Absalom, who rebelled against his father's love and position. He raised an army and came against his father. But David still loved him and his behavior broke David's heart. When the news came that Absalom was dead, we hear the cry of a father's heart as David weeps out, "O my son Absalom, my son, my son Absalom! would God I had died for thee, O Absalom, my son, my son!"

Now Jacob had a son named Joseph. Through the jealousy of his brothers, Joseph was lost to Jacob for many years. The time came when Joseph was the greatest man in Egypt. Hearing that his father was alive, he brought him and all the members of the family down into Egypt and cared for them as long as they lived. Would you rather be an Absalom, breaking your father's heart and bringing him in sorrow to the grave, or would you rather be a Joseph, loving your father and filling his last days with happiness and pride? "Honor thy father and thy mother."

2. *We honor our parents by obeying them.* Paul said that "the powers that be are ordained of God." This is true of all authority, whether it be in the home, the state or the church. God is the absolute Sovereign, but He endowed man with some sovereignty. This is especially true of parents. He clothes them with divine authority. Our parents are God's representatives. They are for us in God's stead. We have no more right to disobey our parents than we have to disobey God.

In Ephesians 6:1 we read, "Children, obey your parents in the Lord: for this is right." Many modern children have changed this verse. They say, "Parents, obey your children, or you will catch trouble." I used to say to my boys, "You may do some things that are wrong because you don't know any better. But when you disobey my direct command, always I will punish you."

Disobedience to parents leads to crime and unhappiness. Let me illustrate. Here is a boy in a certain home and he is not made to obey. The parents say, "We mustn't inhibit him —we mustn't restrain him—we must let him have his own way." So they let him run wild. They never correct him and he becomes a wretched little savage. He is always discontented. He is always demanding something for himself. So instead of being happy, he is abnormal and unhappy. Other children don't want to play with him, because he is too selfish. Other parents dread to see him coming. He becomes a problem child in school and makes the teacher's life miserable. Later he goes out into life. He has never been made to obey at home, so why should he obey the law of the land. What happens? First he is a juvenile delinquent and a little later he is a hardened criminal. The biggest business in America today is the crime business, and the majority of criminals come from homes where no wholesome discipline is known. Every criminal once sat in some mother's lap. Parents, you are doing the worst thing you can do for your children when you don't enforce obedience. Children, you do not like this discipline now, but someday you will thank God that your parents made you obey.

Jesus gave us a beautiful example of obedience to parents. He was the only sinless child born—He never did anything wrong. His mother was Mary and his foster-father was Joseph. They were simply human beings, sinners like us all. Nevertheless, Jesus was always obedient and kind to them.

Is there a time when children are excused from obeying their parents? Yes, when to obey them would be to go against

God's will and God's Word. I know of young men who have felt God's call to preach, but their parents objected strenuously. What are they to do? They are to follow Christ. Our allegiance to Him is our highest allegiance. When a question arises as to following Christ or anyone else in the world, Christ should always come first.

When Jesus was twelve, he went to the Temple in Jerusalem. There he confounded the great religious leaders of His day with His spiritual knowledge. And when His mother found Him there, she began to rebuke Him, but He answered "I must be about my Father's business." This did not mean that he had broken away from them, for the Bible says that He went home with them and was subject unto them. But it did mean that He was putting His Heavenly Father and His business above all else. He said on one occasion that if anyone loved father or mother more than they loved Him, they were not worthy of Him. However, in matters which do not conflict with the divine will of God, children are to obey their parents.

High up in the Rocky Mountains the rains fall upon the Continental Divide. One drop of water goes toward the East, flows down the Mississippi and into the Gulf of Mexico. One drop goes toward the West and ends up in the Pacific Ocean. They start out together, but they end up a continent apart. Two young people start out under the same circumstances. One is disobedient to his parents, the other is affectionately obedient. The time will come when they will be as far apart as the oceans. One will be living a righteous life for God; the other will be wasting his life in selfish endeavor.

Dr. J. A. Campbell was president of Buie's Creek Academy in North Carolina, which later became Campbell College. He tells about taking his two sons to Wake Forest College. They had never been away from home a night in their lives. He went to their room in the dormitory and helped them to get settled. He said it was hard for him to leave his boys, but before he told them good-by, he gave them his check book and said, "When you need anything, just make out a check for it. As long as you live as I have taught you, and as long as you stand for the things that I stand for, I will honor your checks at the bank." He said that money was often scarce, but when the checks came to the bank, somehow he was always able to take care of them. Today his two sons are themselves college presidents. Yes, if a child will be respectful and obedient and live as his godly parents have taught him to live, life will be better for him in every way. So we say that children can honor their parents by being obedient to them. A disobedient child is a drain upon society, a burden upon the state, a stumbling block for the church, and a cause of heartbreak to his parents.

3. *We honor our parents by caring for them in their time of need.* One of the most serious problems of the day concerns what to do with people when they become old and helpless. The heathen races put them out to die. In our own country missionaries to the Indians have saved certain old people who were cast out upon the wastelands to perish. Love is the theme of Christianity, so we can't do a thing like that. Sometimes the old folks are irritable and grouchy, but it is still the duty of the children to care for them.

Jesus found the rule of Corban among the Jews. If a man wanted to be rid of his care for his aged parents, all that he had to say was, "It is Corban." This meant that his money was dedicated to religion and that he would be free of any responsibility for the parents. Jesus blazed out at these religious leaders who taught this principle. He said that they dishonored God and made His Word of none effect. Listen to I Timothy 5:8: "But if any provide not for his own, and specially for those of his own house, he hath denied the faith, and is worse than an infidel."

Our parents loved us in spite of our faults. We should feel the same way about them, especially when they grow old. If we must carry them in our arms, we remember that they carried us. If we must feed them with a spoon, we must remember that they fed us with a spoon. If we must clothe them, we must remember that they clothed us. If we must provide for them, we must remember that they provided for us. Jesus on the Cross provided for His mother and again set an example for us.

A young couple had to take care of their aged parents. The old folks had palsy and when they ate their meals they often dropped food on the tablecloth. So the son made a wooden trough from which they were forced to eat. One day the little boy in the home was seen to be building something. His mother asked him what he was building, and he replied, "I am building a wooden trough for you and daddy to eat out of when you get old and I have to keep you." As Christians we must take care of our parents.

II. THE PARENTS' PART

If the parents expect to be honored, they must be worthy of honor. You can't deceive your children — they know what you are. If you are not what you ought to be, it will be hard for them to honor you. What must you do to win their honor?

1. *The parents must live for Christ.* What were those qualities in your father and mother which held your honor and respect? What was it that brought your soul to its knees as you thought of them? It was not the beauty of your mother, nor the intelligence of your father, but their genuine Christian goodness. So if you parents today want your children

to remember you in the right way, you must live good Christian lives.

When a certain boy went away to college, his mother said to him: "Son, you will have many temptations up there, but remember that each night at 9 o'clock we will be praying for you at the family altar." The boy went to college, lived a clean life and made the football team. The last game of the season was a crucial one, but he was able to break through with a touch-down which won the game. That night the coach said to them, "Boys, you have been training all season — you have had to be in bed at 10 o'clock each night — I am taking the restrictions off tonight. Go out and have a good time." The boys went out to paint the town red and to end up in a house of prostitution. Soon they were swinging down the street together. Suddenly a clock chimed nine times. This boy said, "Boys, I can't go with you into sin. My folks are at home right now praying for me. I can't go, boys, I can't do it." That is the kind of home and parents which will bring a boy back when temptations assail him.

2. *Parents must lead their children to Christ.* You want your children to have good physical health, but what about their spiritual health? You call the doctor when your children are physically sick. Do you pray when they are spiritually sick? You want them to learn the things of the world. How about the things of God? You want them well clothed. Are they clothed in the righteousness of Christ? You would do anything to save your children from physical death. Are you doing anything to save them from spiritual death? The Bible tells us to bring up our children in the "nurture and admonition of the Lord." This means that we are to begin early by telling them Bible stories and teaching them of Christ and their need of Him. It means taking them to church and Sun-

day school. It means leading them to Christ when they come to the age of accountability.

A woman sat at her window one spring day watching a mother bird as she built her nest on a bush which hung near the ground. "Ah, my tiny friend," she said, "you are building too low." She went out and tore the nest down, but the bird insisted on coming back and building the nest in the same low place. Soon there were several eggs in the nest and later there were several little baby birds. One day the woman heard the distressed cry of the mother bird, and as she ran to the window, she saw that a serpent had found the nest and was devouring the little birds. The mother bird had built too low.

Parents are often guilty of the same thing. They build upon the things of this world. They give their time and attention to the clubs and organizations of the world, and soon the world comes in and destroys their children. Oh, mothers and fathers, build high for your children's sake. Build on Christ, build on prayer, build on the Bible and the church. Then you will be worthy of the honor of your children.

III. The Promise

That thy days may be long upon the land which the Lord thy God giveth thee.

As we see Israel marching toward the Promised Land, we wonder how long they can stay there. God promised them that they could live there forever. But to enjoy this rich heritage of grace it was necessary for them to walk in obedience, both before God and His representatives — their parents. There is a double duty enjoined here and it applies to the day in which we live. Just because you are good to your parents doesn't guarantee that you are going to be blessed here and that you are going to heaven. You must serve both God and your parents.

Do we want to have a great, strong nation, blessed of God? Then we must have children who honor and obey their parents. This is what God meant in His promise. The right kind of children will become the right kind of citizens. The right kind of Christian citizens will bring the blessing of God upon our nation. Our nation's security depends not upon our military might, but upon the character of our people. A nation of obedient, God-fearing, parent-honoring people can expect the blessing of God upon it.

Here is an illustration from the Book of Jeremiah. The Rechabites were offered wine to drink, but they turned it down. They said that they had promised their father that they would never touch strong drink. They honored him by obeying him. Then God said, "Because you honor your father in this way, your family will stand before me forever." This promise has been wonderfully fulfilled. In 1862, hundreds of years after the promise, a tribe of Rechabites was found living near the Dead Sea.

When you find a young man today who rightly honors his mother and father, it is likely that he will have in him those traits of character which lead to happiness and success. George Washington was getting ready to go to sea as a midshipman. His trunk was already on the vessel and he was telling his mother good-by. When he saw that his departure was causing her great sorrow, he called a servant and said, "Go and bring my trunk back." His mother said to him, "God has promised to bless the children who honor their parents, and I believe that He will bless you." And every American knows that God kept that promise in the case of George Washington.

Have you fallen short of honoring your parents? Well, there is forgiveness for you. Come and confess your sins to God and go out to make up to your parents what you have lacked of loving service. It is said that in China every son takes a present to his parents on New Year's morning. He thanks them for what they have done in the past, and prays for a continuance of their affection. We ought to live in that spirit every day.

But the best way for us to make our parents happy is to live our lives for Christ in such a way as to make them proud of us. In fact, you can never keep this commandment, nor any other, unless you let Jesus have His way in your heart and life.

My wish for myself is also my wish for every mother and father in this congregation. When my work is done and God calls me away, I want my boys to come and look down into my face and be able to say, "Daddy didn't leave us a million dollars, but he did leave the memory of a good life spent in the service of the Lord Jesus Christ." This is the greatest heritage that we can leave our children.

When Dr. Robert G. Lee, the great preacher of Memphis, was a young man, he went to Panama to work and to make enough money to finish college. Before he left, his mother put her hands upon his shoulders, looked into his eyes and said, "Bob, you will be gone from home a long time. But when you come back I am going to look into your eyes and I can tell whether or not you have dishonored your mother and your God." The young man went to Panama and faced many temptations, but he kept himself clean. When he came home to South Carolina and met his mother, he put his hands upon her shoulders and said, "Mother, look into my eyes. I have lived clean and straight. I never took a drink, I never gambled, I never touched a woman." His mother looked and was satisfied.

Oh, may God help us so to live that when we meet our mothers and fathers in another world, we shall be able to say, "I lived every day for your Savior and mine."

Sermon 6

THOU SHALT NOT KILL

Thou shalt not kill (Exodus 20:13).

This commandment faces man with the sacredness of human life. We are living in an age when it seems that the life of others is lightly regarded. Around the world thousands of people are starving; thousands are being ushered into eternity. We read about these things in our paper and promptly forget them. We eat our good meals, we sleep in our soft beds, we wear our good clothes, we look at our television sets and go to the various places of amusement, and think nothing of the world's tragedies. Loss of life doesn't seem to bother us unless it is right in our own homes.

Charles Wellborn tells of an artist who set up a statue of a boy for exhibition. He put some bright lights on the floor, so that these lights would shine up into the boy's face. When he stepped back and looked at the statue the face of the boy looked like the face of a moron. He then changed the lights and put them above the statue. This time when he looked at the boy's face, it appeared to be the face of an angel. So it is that when we look at men from our standpoint, they look like mere animals. We say, "What is the difference? What does it matter if these people die?" But God looks down from above and sees humanity with a different eye. A man is precious in His sight. He may be poor and ugly and wicked, just one of the two and a half billion people in the world. But God looks upon him as a most valuable treasure.

When God created the world and all that is in it, He said, "Let us make man in our own image." So He made man like Himself and put him down into the world. Then when that man had gone astray, God said, I still love him, and I will give My Only-begotten Son to save him. Out on dark Calvary the rich, red, ruby, royal blood of the Son of God was poured out for man's redemption. Yes, I tell you, man is precious in God's sight. No wonder God says, You must not kill him; you must not destroy him.

This is the shortest of the commandments and yet it is the strongest of all. Society will forgive a man for being an atheist, an idolater, a profane man, a Sabbath-breaker or one who dishonors his parents. Men will even condone an adulterer and a thief, a false witness or a covetous man. But when one man willfully and deliberately robs another of his life, the whole world considers this as the greatest of all evils.

Now in order to understand the full meaning of this commandment, let me say that the translation should be, not "thou shalt not kill," but "thou shalt do no murder." There is a vast difference in the two. In this sermon I will seek to show you that killing is not always a crime in God's sight, but murder is always the worst of crimes.

I. Things Not Forbidden In This Commandment

1. *God doesn't forbid the killing of animals for food or clothing, or some other useful purpose.* We will start at the lower level and proceed to the higher. When Noah and his family came out of the ark, God saw that they needed food, so He said, "Every moving thing that liveth shall be meat for you" (Gen. 9:3). Right there God was giving man permission to kill animals and birds for his own use. You see,

God felt man was more important than any other creature He had made. In Old Testament times thousands of rams, lambs and doves were killed and offered as sacrifices under the instructions of God. When Jesus was here He ate the passover lamb and provided fish for Himself and the disciples and the people to eat. In the story of the prodigal son He speaks of killing the fatted calf.

Not only does this commandment permit us to kill animals for food, but also animals of prey, like the lion, the tiger or the bear. David slew a lion and a bear and this is often done today as a matter of protection.

2. *God does not forbid the killing of a thief who breaks into your home.* "If a thief be found breaking up, and be smitten that he die, there shall no blood be shed for him" (Ex. 22:2). This simply means that if I awake in the middle of the night and a thief has broken into my house to steal my property, I have a right to shoot him and no punishment will come to me because of it. The law of our land recognizes this same principle. While the law permits it, as a Christian I could never feel right in my conscience about it. It is a serious thing to send a soul into eternity.

Then there is the matter of self-defense. Suppose a man in hot anger comes against you to kill you. You have every right to protect yourself. If the other man is killed you are not to blame. However, let us pray God that we shall never be placed in the position where we are forced to shed the blood of another.

3. *Killing in war is not forbidden here.* Many service men have been disturbed about this matter. They have gone into battle and they know without a doubt that they have killed another man. They ask the question, "Am I a murderer?" The answer is, "No, you are not a murderer."

In the first place, we are citizens of a nation—we are subject to the powers which are ordained of God. We do not want war, but when the federal head of the nation declares war, we must obey. If in so obeying we kill an enemy, I do not believe that would be classed as murder.

This does not mean that war is right—it can't be. War sheds the blood of innocent millions. It makes orphans and widows of once happy people. It brings starvation and sufferin. It costs billions! Most of our tax money goes for wars, money which could bless the world. Yet it never results in anything good. But as long as there is sin in the world we are going to have war. One group of people may be peaceful and God-loving. Then there comes a time when a Godless nation attacks them. These good people must fight for their lives, their freedom, their homes and loved ones, and their churches. So I would say that if you are on the side of such a nation, if you fight and kill, you are not a murderer. But suppose you are on the side of the guilty nation. I am sure that some good Christians fought for Japan, they were forced to. Well, they had to obey the powers ordained of God, therefore they are not murderers. No, the murderers are the war-mongers, who thrust their countries into war.

It is true that God's people, Israel, were commanded to fight the nations of Canaan. Why did God command this? Simply because they were God's enemies. The cup of their sin was overflowing and God had to punish them. But today you can't justify war on the grounds of Israel's wars in the Old Testament. They received a direct command from God; we do not receive such commands. I am afraid that the wars of today are never justified. But it is not the soldier's fault if he kills another. He is simply obeying the powers that be and God will not hold him guilty.

I recently read a sermon which was preached in 1889. The preacher said that we were becoming more highly civilized and that the time would soon come when mankind would rule out war altogether. Since that time the bloodiest wars of all time have been fought. Bible-believing Christians look forward to the time when Christ returns and takes over. Then wars will cease, swords will be beaten into plowshares, spears will be turned into pruning-hooks and the nations will study war no more.

4. *Capital punishment is not forbidden.* God said in Genesis 9:6: "Whoso sheddeth man's blood, by man shall his blood be shed: for in the image of God made he man." Why does God approve capital punishment? Because man is made in the image of God and no man has a right to lay hand on God's image and go unpunished.

The New Testament contains the same truth. Why did not Jesus miraculously deliver the thief on the cross? Because He knew that this man deserved to die. So when the state kills a man in the electric chair for some heinous crime, the man who pulls the switch is not a murderer.

II. Murder In The Biblical Sense

1. *Let us look at direct murder.* This means deliberately going out after a man to take his life by violence. Every paper that you read tells of such cases. The number of such crimes increases every year. Why? Because men are putting God out of their lives and permitting Satan to take over. Who was the first murderer? You will say that it was Cain. No, Jesus tells us in John 8:44 that Satan was a murderer from the beginning. He is the father of all murderers. Yes, Cain was the first human murderer — in a jealous rage he slew his own brother. Since the time of Cain, hundreds of thousands, ruled by Satan, have killed their victims. Life is sacred and must never be willfully destroyed.

We have made great progress in civilization, in science,

in learning. We prate about our humanitarian service, our charity, our regard for others. Yet, because we still have sin in our hearts, we kill our fellow man. Again we see positive proof that it is not the outside things which change a man, but the presence of Christ in a man's heart.

Mob-murder is also forbidden in this commandment. We thank God that there are fewer lynchings today than in former years. A man is a murderer if he joins with a mob to kill another man. A mob has no right to usurp the functions of a court of justice.

Suicide also comes under the head of murder. Many a man makes a mess of his life through his own folly. He doesn't have the courage to face reality, so he dodges out of life by suicide, leaving the burden which he should have borne on someone else.

Sometimes suicide is committed by those whose minds become unbalanced and whose reason is dethroned. In these cases we may suspend judgment. Some years ago I listened to a wonderful preacher through a series of revival meetings. I have never heard a better Bible scholar in my life. He almost knew the Bible from memory. A few weeks after the meeting this preacher committed suicide. I am sure that his mind was unbalanced and that he could not be classed as a murderer.

But when a man is rational, to commit suicide is to commit murder. When God said, "Thou shalt not murder," He included all of human life. I went one day with another preacher to talk to a man about accepting Christ. This man's wife and two children were members of my church. He turned us down cold — he didn't seem to be concerned about his soul's welfare. Some days later this man went into the bank, entered a small room, and putting the pistol to his temple he committed suicide. I believe that this was a case of murder. The most prominent suicide in the Old Testament was Saul. The most prominent suicide in the New Testament was Judas. You know what kind of men they were.

Then there is infanticide. This is a delicate subject. It simply means abortion. The unborn infant is a person and no one has a right to take its life. This is a secret and silent sin, but God knows about it. Whatever the excuse, this sin is cruel and heartless. The Bible tells us that children are blessings from God. Today they are often considered as domestic nuisances and social inconveniences. Some women are so given over to society and pleasure that they don't want to be bothered with children. But you are to be careful not to break the sixth commandment in this way.

2. *Let us look next at indirect murder.* Here is the part of this commandment which applies to the majority of us. While we do not deliberately kill someone, we can by indirect action bring death to another. You can easily break this law without getting arrested.

You are guilty of indirect murder when you lead someone into sin. A certain man died a drunkard's death. His friend said, "I killed him. I led him into dissipation. I was strong enough to take it, but he was not. I killed him." I believe that the man was right.

One Saturday night in a cafe in the mountains, two young men who had been drinking heavily began shooting at each other. They were both killed and another young man who was in the cafe was also killed. I conducted the funeral for two of these young men. After one of these funerals a wise old man said to me, "Preacher, we will continue to have such sorrow as long as the fathers in this community drink whiskey and carry guns." The parents were guilty of the death of these boys — guilty because they set the wrong example.

The liquor-mongers of today are indirect murderers. Most

of our traffic deaths occur between midnight and four o'clock in the morning. The officials tell us that liquor is involved in the majority of these cases. Men sell liquor for the money that is in it. A man drinks too much and in his drunken stupor he kills another. Whose fault is it? Another man drinks too much, he drives his car under the influence of whiskey and a wreck is the result. Several lives may be lost. Not only is this man a murderer, but the men who made and sold the liquor are also murderers.

You can kill others by the way you live. Years ago I knew a woman whose husband had been a drunkard during the early days of their marriage. She knew the trouble and sorrow which comes from a union of this kind. She had two sons. She told me that she said this to them, "Before you take your first drink, come home and kill me."

A certain father had two sons. They came home drunk at two o'clock in the morning. The father handed each of them a pistol. They were immediately sober and asked their father why he was doing this. He said to them, "Go upstairs and kill your mother! It would be easier on her for you to kill her with these pistols than to kill her by inches as you are doing." Yes, you can kill your loved ones by the way that you live.

You can kill others by neglecting to do the right thing. A tenement house burned down recently killing a family of nine. The firemen testified that the house was a firetrap. The owner was glad to get the rent from the house, but his neglect caused the death of nine people. I don't have time in this message to dwell upon it, but I can say that we often kill the ones we love by neglecting to give them the kindness and thoughtfulness that they deserve.

You can kill yourself by the wrong way of living. The man who digs his grave with his teeth is guilty. The man who engages in anything which brings on premature death is guilty. Dr. Clovis Chappell tells of a friend who said to him, "I have a tobacco heart. The doctor says if I keep on smoking it will kill me. I quit for a while, but I missed it so much that I made up my mind that I would rather die than to deny myself the pleasure of smoking." A lady sat on the other side of my desk the other day and said to me, "I quit smoking some time ago and it is like being freed from prison."

A man who drinks to excess is shortening his own life. Oh, many we have seen who killed everything good in themselves by drinking! They hurt others and finally drank themselves into an early grave. That is murder.

3. *Then there is the spirit of murder.* In the Ten Commandments the overt act is forbidden. When Jesus came, He not only forbade murder, but the spirit which prompts it. "Ye have heard that it was said by them of old time, Thou shalt not kill; and whosoever shall kill shall be in danger of the judgment: But I say unto you, That whosoever is angry with his brother without a cause shall be in danger of the judgment" (Matt. 5:21-22).

Jesus is saying here that we should keep murder out of the heart. That is where sin comes from. You don't have to shoot a man to be a murderer; you have violated this commandment if you have murder in your heart. You will fare no better at the judgment than the man whose hands are gory with human blood.

Some people live lives of hatred. Every time they think of certain persons, they boil over with indignation. They wish for these others every conceivable hurt, even unto death. In the eyes of the law they are not guilty, because they have shed no blood. But not so with God. He looketh on the heart and He counts them guilty of murder if they have murder in their heart.

Do you want to know whether or not you are saved? "Whosoever hateth his brother is a murderer: and ye know that no murderer hath eternal life abiding in him," says I John 3:15. This Scripture plainly states that if you hate anyone you don't have eternal life.

Do you have the right to punish those who wrong you? No, that right belongs to God. "Dearly beloved, avenge not yourselves, but rather give place unto wrath: for it is written, Vengeance is mine; I will repay, saith the Lord" (Rom. 12:19). If someone has wronged you, you're not to try to get even with them. You are to leave that to God. He can do a better job than you can. He is taking care of the matter. He may not do it today or tomorrow, but in His own good time He will handle it. It is your place to keep clean and to leave all to God.

III. Now Think Of Murder Of The Soul

1. *This may occur in the home.* Godless parents who never teach their children about Christ and never take them to church may someday meet their children in hell. There the children will point an accusing finger at them and say, "We are here because you murdered our souls by your godless example."

2. *This may occur in school.* Many of our young people have gone to certain schools, and under the influence of godless teachers and infidel teaching, they have turned their backs upon God forever. God help the teacher who tampers with the souls of his pupils.

3. *This may occur in the church.* The modernistic preacher makes light of the Bible, denies the Virgin Birth and laughs at the idea of heaven, hell and the judgment. Those who hear and believe him never come by faith to Christ, consequently they are forever lost. Their souls have been murdered.

4. *This may occur through your influence.* Someone looks up to you and believes you and follows you. If your life is not consistently Christian, it causes that one to turn aside from God. You cause that one to lose his soul.

You may murder your own soul. Soul-suicide is worse than body-suicide. Christ knocks at the door of your heart again and again. When you turn Him away, you murder your own soul and sentence it to an eternal death.

Dr. Robert Stuart McArthur was for many years pastor of the Calvary Baptist Church, New York City. After the service on Sunday night a man asked him this question. "Dr. McArthur, if I give my heart to Christ, will I be forced to give up my money?" Dr. McArthur replied, "I do not know. If God tells you to give it up, you must do that." This man, who happened to be wealthy, said, "I will think about this matter during the week, and give you my answer next Sunday night." The next Sunday night the man came back to Dr. McArthur and said, "Preacher, if Christ and heaven must go, I will simply have to let them go. I am going to hold on to my money." This man was committing soul suicide.

IV. The Greatest Murder Of All

This murder took place 1900 years ago. It was committed just outside the city walls of Jerusalem. On the blackest Friday that ever dawned, the sweet, sinless, wonderful Son of God was murdered upon a cruel Roman cross.

I love that old spiritual, "Were you there when they crucified my Lord?" You will say, "No, I wasn't there. I hadn't been born." Ah, but you and I were there. We were represented at the Cross by our sins. The Cross would never have been raised if it hadn't been for our sins. We cut down the tree, we laid the stripes upon His back, we drove the spikes into His hands and feet, we thrust the spear into His side. We murdered Jesus — not the Roman soldiers, not the Jewish leaders. They were just instruments — you and I slew the Son of God.

But thank God, there is forgiveness for us. If you will come repenting of your sins, confessing Christ and trusting Him, the same blood which we spilt when we crucified Christ will cover our sins and will pass us from death unto life. God said that He would bury our sin in the deepest sea, that He would put it behind His back, that He would put it as far away from us as the east is from the west. Thank God, there is mercy and grace and salvation in Him.

How can we keep this commandment? Not in our own strength — we must have Jesus in our hearts. Hatred and Jesus cannot dwell in the same heart. So I bid you to come to Him today and let Him fill your heart with grace and power.

One night we were having dinner in the home of some friends in the Deep South. When the colored cook served the meal, I asked her about her faith in Christ and her church membership. In replying to me, she said, "The main thing is to keep plenty of Jesus in your heart." My friends, this is true. He is your greatest need. If He is already your Savior, let Him have full sway in your life. If He is not your Savior, why not let Him come into your heart right now.

Sermon 7

THOU SHALT NOT COMMIT ADULTERY

Thou shalt not commit adultery (Exodus 20:14).

This commandment has nothing pretty about it. The very use of the word "adultery" brings black thoughts to our minds. We wish that we could skip over this commandment. We wish that we could be silent about sexual matters. We wish that we didn't have to bring these things out into the open. But God knew that the sexual urge was the strongest of human instincts. He knew all the trouble and tragedies that could arise from the wrong use of sex. So we hear Him saying, not only to Israel, but to all the world, "Thou shalt not commit adultery."

In the early days of my ministry I preached a sermon on Rahab. I mentioned the fact that she was a harlot. After the service a man declared that I had insulted every woman present by using the word "harlot." There are still many people who feel that the preacher ought not speak out plainly on these matters, especially when young people are present. But I feel that we have neglected our duty along these lines too long. We need to speak out on these vital questions. Too many of our young people are going astray today. They are indulging in promiscuous sex activities, bringing shame and disgrace and trouble upon themselves and upon all those who love them. A man who recently wrote the story of his own life of folly and sin, said that he attributed his sinful deeds to the fact that he had never heard a sermon on the seventh commandment.

A college student said to a minister, "I am having some intellectual difficulties with the Bible." The minister listened patiently while the young man told of his doubts and difficulties. Then the preacher said, "Charlie, is your life pure?" Finally the young man admitted that it was not. The preacher then said, "There may be some difficult passages in the Bible which are hard to understand, but the Bible is certainly quite plain on the seventh commandment."

"Some of the ten commandments may seem to be musty and out-of-date," says one of our preachers, "but not so with the seventh commandment. It is as modern as the story of infidelity and immorality which you read about in your morning newspaper." There has been a tremendous moral letdown in our country in the last thirty-five years. The relationship between the sexes is more lax than at any time in our history. Therefore, if a preacher is to preach to his day and generation, he must sound the trumpet on the matter of adultery and immorality. He must echo the thunders of Sinai, "Thou shalt not commit adultery."

Elton Trueblood, the Quaker preacher, says, "The most obvious form that a rotten civilization takes is in an absurd emphasis on sexual pleasures, both in practice and literature." Go back down the corridors of history. Think of Rome and the other great nations which came tumbling down into oblivion. What will you find as the basic cause? You will find that sex was glorified and immorality ran riot. Well, look at our beloved America. Look at some of the picture shows, look at the plays which run the longest in New York, look at the magazine covers. You see the same thing—sex is glorified.

It seems that Satan is using every method known to man to-day to pull us down into the cesspool of sexual sin, to get us to break the seventh commandment.

In order to have a best seller today, it is almost imperative for the author to fill the pages with filth. He must always present several illicit sex experiences in the book. Then he knows it will sell. This shows how low we've sunk in morality. Surely, we must be living in those perilous times which Paul described would come in the last days.

I. God's Arrangement for Man's Well-Being

God does not deny sex and the sex urge. The Bible teaches that there is nothing wrong with sex; it is not immoral. There is nothing wrong with it in its right relationship. God ordained sex for a purpose — a good purpose. He gave it to us for the purpose of replenishing the earth. When we keep it in place, it is a great blessing. When we use it wrongly, it becomes a terrible master which sends men and women to hell.

Now God protected the purpose of sex by ordaining the institution of marriage. For a moment let's go back to the Garden of Eden. It is the sixth day of the creative week. Adam, fresh from the hand of God, walks through the Garden, lord of all he surveys. But somehow he is ill at ease; something is lacking. God senses Adam's feelings, so he causes all the animals and all the birds to come trooping by Adam. Adam gives a name to each one of them, but among all of them he does not find a true mate, a true companion. Now God causes a deep sleep to fall upon Adam. We can see him lying on the velvet grass of the Garden. God then performs the first surgical operation. He takes a rib from the side of Adam, closes up the wound and out of this rib makes the first woman. In a few minutes Adam awakens from sleep. He rubs his eyes as he looks upon a vision fairer than all the birds and beasts of the garden. Immediately he falls in love with this fair creature. They stand before God in this beautiful Garden, while the birds sing the wedding music and heaven looks on; God joins them in holy wedlock.

I begin my wedding ceremony by saying, "Marriage is the fitting sign and seal of love. It is one of the good and perfect gifts which cometh down from our Father in heaven, with whom there is no variableness nor shadow that is made by turning. When God created the first woman He brought her to the first man and she became his wife. Since that time in every age and in every nation men and women have been joined together in the holy bonds of matrimony. We therefore justly believe that every true marriage is ordained in heaven, before it is consummated on earth." Yes, marriage is one of the oldest gifts to mankind. It antedates the entrance of sin into the world. It was God's eternal plan to create a human family. He began this family with one man and one woman. That was His plan for the first family and His plan for every family. And in ordaining marriage, He throws a protecting screen around the sex life and provides for its rightful use.

Genesis 2:24 in the Old Testament and Ephesians 5:31 in the New Testament are practically the same, "For this cause shall a man leave his father and mother, and be joined unto his wife, and they two shall be one flesh." For what cause? For the cause of creating a family; the cause of replenishing the race, the cause of protecting and purifying the sex urge. Marriage is God's plan for us. It is the highest human relationship. It makes the wedded pair one. God meant for it to be a permanent arrangement.

There is only one Biblical basis for marriage, and that is love, the peculiar love which God puts into the bosom of a man and woman. To marry for any other purpose is not to be truly married. A marriage built on any other foundation will fail. Some marry because they are lonely, some for social position, some for money, some to get away from an unpleasant situation, some because of fleshly desires, and others marry because they have been jilted and they want to get even with the one who jilted them. But I say again, if you don't come to the marriage altar with the tenderest love in your heart, one for the other, you can't expect a happy marriage. Love is the only basis for marriage.

I have heard of couples who danced and drank until the early hours of the morning, then in a drunken stupor they went to a justice of the peace and had him marry them. That is not a case of "what God has joined together," but a case of what Satan had joined together.

Why is love such a necessary basis for a successful marriage? Because the pathway of life is strewn with many trials and hardships. It takes a mutual love and understanding to hold a couple together. If love is not there, the bonds of matrimony are easily broken. But someone says, "We will marry and maybe love will come later." That is a tremendous mistake. If either party plans to come to the marriage altar without a deep love in his or her heart, that party owes it to himself and to the other party to stay out of marriage.

Jacob worked seven years to get his beloved Rachel, and we read that these seven years seemed but a few days because of the love which he had for her. If our marriages were based on a love like that, all the years would be sweet and wonderful.

Paul tells us to marry "in the Lord." This means that a Christian is not to be married to an unbeliever. Again he says, "Be ye not unequally yoked together with unbelievers." I have heard girls say, "I know he is not a Christian, but after we marry I am sure I can change him." They are wrong. A woman assumes a hard job when she tries to reform a man after marriage. It hardly ever happens. If he swears before marriage, he will swear after marriage. If he comes to see you with liquor on his breath before marriage, he will drink after marriage. If his conduct is unchristian before marriage, it will be unchristian after marriage.

I have witnessed this tragedy over and over. One afternoon I performed a marriage ceremony for a certain couple. The girl was a church member, but the man was not. I talked to them about this matter, and she put her hand through his arm and said, "I am going to bring him to church every Sunday." But it didn't turn out that way. Soon they drifted away and neither one ever came to church. It was just the case of a Christian going against the will of God. Billy Graham said, "If I married a woman and she did not know Christ, I would never be able to trust her all the way, because an unregenerate heart outside of Christ is potentially capable of any sin."

Now let me warn you against mixed marriages. The only way to have a happy marriage is to have the big things of life in common. If the wife is a Protestant and the husband a Catholic or vice versa, they will be miles apart in the most important area of their lives. What usually happens in such a case? Either one party must make a sacrifice where precious values are concerned, or both of them give up spiritual things altogether. These differences lead to tremendous complications in the home, and the children are the ones who have to pay the price and bear the evil results. So I would say to all young people, marry only the one who has the same spiritual things in common with you. The best way to avoid trouble is not to date one whose religious views are so different from yours. You don't have to be "snooty" about it — just quietly break up such alliances before you become entangled.

Now you have seen God's wonderful and blessed arrangement for a man and a woman, for the family and for the home. Marriage is God's way of protecting society, propagating the race and bringing happiness to mankind.

II. Man's Departure From God's Plan

Yes, God made arrangements for the proper use of sex. But man is a sinful being and he departed from God's plan. This is the reason that God gave man the seventh commandment, "Thou shalt not commit adultery." But this is not the only Scripture against it. There are warnings against adultery in all parts of the Bible.

> *Job 31:11:* For this is an heinous crime; yea, it is an iniquity to be punished by the judges. For it is a fire that consumeth to destruction.
>
> *Proverbs 6:27-29:* Can a man take fire in his bosom, and his clothes not be burned? Can one go upon hot coals, and his feet not be burned? So he that goeth in to his neighbour's wife; whosoever toucheth her shall not be innocent.
>
> *Proverbs 6:32:* But whoso committeth adultery with a woman lacketh understanding: he that doeth it destroyeth his own soul.
>
> *I Corinthians 6:9:* Know ye not that the unrighteous shall not inherit the kingdom of God? Be not deceived: neither fornicators, nor idolaters, nor adulterers, nor effeminate, nor abusers of themselves with mankind . . . shall inherit the kingdom of God.
>
> *Ephesians 5:3:* But fornication and all uncleanness, or covetousness, let it not be once named among you, as becometh saints.
>
> *Revelation 21:8:* But the fearful, and unbelieving, and the abominable, and murderers, and whoremongers, and sorcerers, and idolaters, and all liars, shall have their part in the lake which burneth with fire and brimstone: which is the second death.

We go back to Leviticus 20:10 and we hear God pronouncing the death penalty upon both the adulterer and the adulteress. "And the man that committeth adultery with another man's wife, even he that committeth adultery with his neighbour's wife, the adulterer and the adulteress shall surely be put to death." If this law prevailed today, there would be millions of funerals.

In the Book of Proverbs we are told that the steps of an impure woman lead to death and take hold on hell. Again we are told that the man who goes to her house and commits adultery lands in hell. Over and over God repeats this same truth. There are six Scriptures in the Bible which tell us that adultery is the way to hell. This does not mean that every man who has committed adultery will go to hell, any more than every man who lies will go to hell. But it means that if a man keeps on this sinful course and will not come to the cleansing fountain of Jesus' blood, he will surely land in hell.

But God has a punishment for this sin right here. The sins that a man commits are punished in his body while he is yet upon this earth. For instance the drunkard suffers cirrhosis of the liver, and other punishments. But no sin in the world brings such suffering as often results from adultery. I am speaking now of venereal disease. God hates adultery. That is the reason he punishes it so severely right here. A man and woman never know when they are going to contract this disease, all because they break God's commandments for a moment of pleasure.

One morning when Jesus was in the Temple a group of self-righteous scribes and Pharisees brought before him a woman taken in the act of adultery. Do you wonder why they did not also bring the man? Well, she was guilty and according to the law she deserved to die. These men tried to trap Jesus, but He simply knelt and wrote on the ground. I can imagine that they said, "Come on, what are you going to do with her?" And Jesus looking up, said, "He that is without sin, let him be the first one to cast a stone." He kept writing on the ground while these men looked over his shoulder. Their faces turned red and soon the last one was gone. What did Jesus write on the ground? Maybe He wrote the seventh commandment. These men knew that they were guilty and they couldn't condemn the woman. Jesus forgave this woman. Have you ever come to Him for the forgiveness of your sin?

Adultery has a degrading effect upon character. All that is decent and fine goes down the drain when you commit adultery, and a feeling of shame and uncleanness envelops the adulterer. He hesitates to pray—he turns his back upon God's house. He takes the trail that leads down to other sins. There is nothing uplifting about adultery.

A man who commits some other sin can say, "This is my own private business." But sexual sins are different. They affect other people; they harm other people. They involve trifling with human affections and loyalties. Often they bring a new life into the world. The sixth and the seventh commandments are closely related. "Thou shalt not kill" and "thou shalt not commit adultery." They both involve the sacredness of human personality. It is wrong to kill the body by murder; it is wrong to soil and degrade the body by adultery.

The question of divorce is involved here, also. This evil has grown to vast proportions today. A few years ago divorce was considered a disgrace; now one out of three marriages ends in divorce. There are those who flit from husband to husband and from wife to wife, as a bird flits from one branch of the tree to the other. And not all of this is confined to Hollywood. What does Jesus say about it? He says that the only ground for divorce is adultery, the breaking of the seventh commandment. This shows how serious sin is in God's sight. Adultery is the only thing that kills the marriage contract. The husband may be a drunkard, the wife may nag, the house may look like a pig-pen, but these are not causes for divorce. Adultery is the Biblical cause. Couples have a right to separate but they have no right to marry again unless adultery has been involved.

Jesus said, "What . . . God hath joined together, let no man put asunder." Man has no authority to separate a husband and wife unless they have God's permission. He gives this permission if this command has been broken. Where does the divorce hurt most? In the lives of the children. Untold misery and calamity is brought upon them. Court officials tell us that the majority of criminals come from broken homes.

I have talked often to couples who were contemplating divorce. In some cases several children were involved. I have said to them. "Maybe the wife has done wrong; maybe the husband has done wrong. But the children are innocent bystanders. They didn't ask to be brought into the world. You may not love each other any more, but for the children's sake, you ought to keep the home together and do the best that you can for them."

Dr. John R. Rice tells us that there are at least three actions which can lead a person to commit adultery. First, the modern dance. Some young people don't understand, but any mature person who knows about the human body and human passions, knows that this is true. Many prostitutes testify that the modern dance, with the close contact of bodies and indecent exposure of the feminine form, led them into sin. Men and women are so built that dancing can set the body on fire and incite human passions.

Then Dr. Rice mentions indecent movies. I am sure that not all movies are filled with sex, but many of them are. And we do know that many actors and actresses are living in legalized adultery. Several years ago the Payne Foundation selected a number of the most prominent educators in America to investigate the movies. They checked 1,500 pictures and reported that the principal theme in the majority of them was sex. If boys and girls drink these scenes in through the eyes week after week, it is bound to do harm and lower their moral resistance.

Dr. Rice mentions petting as another action which can lead to adultery. When boys and girls take liberties in fondling and handling and caressing each others' bodies, they may be on the road which leads to the scarlet sin. While Dr. Rice was holding a meeting in a Texas church, one night a girl sought him out and told him a sad story. She went to the country club dance with Bob. She loved him and was engaged to marry him. But that night she also danced with Bill. He held her close and after one of the dances he said, "Let's sit this one out." They went out on the porch and he said, "Let's sit in my car." They got into the car and soon they had parked in a country lane. . . . As the girl told her story she began to sob, and said, "Preacher, I am going to have a baby. What am I going to do . . . . I don't want to murder the baby. . . . I can't tell Bob, it will break his heart and he won't marry me. I don't love Bill and I don't want to marry him. Preacher, what am I going to do?"

Every pastor could tell you many stories of sad and tragic results which occurred when this commandment was broken. Listen, young people, someday you are going to meet "the one and only." You will want to marry him or her. You are going to expect your mate to be clean and pure and above reproach. All right, they will have the right to expect the same of you. Be sure to keep yourself clean and pure for the man or woman you are someday going to choose to walk down life's pathway with you.

The Bible has several things to say to a Christian which apply right here. "But ye are washed, but ye are sanctified, but ye are justified in the name of our Lord Jesus" (I Cor. 6:11). Because you have been washed in the blood of Christ, you must live a pure life. Verse 13 says, "The body is not for fornication, but for the Lord." The body is to be used for Him, and not for sin.

"Know ye not that your bodies are the members of Christ? shall I then take the members of Christ, and make them the members of an harlot? God forbid. What? know ye not that he which is joined to an harlot is one body? for two, saith he, shall be one flesh" (I Cor. 6:15-16). If we are joined to Christ, we have no right to bring adultery into the relationship. In verse 19 Paul says that the body is the temple of the Holy Spirit. In other words, God lives in us and His dwelling place ought not to be profaned.

I want you to think of two Old Testament characters, both of them men of God. Both of them were tempted by the same sin. David saw Bath-sheba and sent for her and committed adultery with her. Joseph was fiercely tempted by Potiphar's wife but he turned away from her, saying, "This will be a sin against God. I can't do it." What was the final result of these two decisions. David sinned and the sword never departed from his house. Sorrow piled upon sorrow for him. But Joseph went on to become the prime minister of Egypt. Sin pays off in one way; virtue pays off in another.

I have been talking about the act of adultery. But Jesus said that this sin could be committed in our minds. "Ye have heard that it was said by them of old time, Thou shalt not commit adultery: But I say unto you, That whosoever looketh on a woman to lust after her hath committed adultery with her already in his heart" (Matt. 5:27, 28). Here God's Son, pure of heart and life, tells us that we can violate the seventh commandment not only in the outward bodily act, but in the inward unclean desire. Keep your heart clean and in close contact with Christ and this sin will have no dominion over you.

You can't help but look the first time, but it is the second look which is wrong. It is then that the heart imagines sin; it is then that the soul becomes soiled with evil. You can't keep the birds from flying over your head, but you can keep them from roosting in your hair. When evil thoughts come, don't let them stay. Drive them out with pure and noble thoughts of Christ and righteousness.

Hebrews 13:4 tells us that God will judge whoremongers and adulterers, not only those who commit the bodily act, but those who commit adultery in their hearts. In Romans 1 Paul speaks of this very sin. Three times he says that God "gave them up" to this sin. If you continue in this sin, God can't do anything else but give you up.

III. Christ's Remedy For This Sin

You know the remedy — the only remedy. If you have broken this commandment, come to Christ. Tell Him all about it. Tell Him that you want to give it up. Ask Him to forgive you and help you. And I guarantee that He will say to you as He said to the woman, "Go, and sin no more." He wouldn't have told her that if He hadn't been willing to give her the Holy Spirit to help her keep clean. He will do the same thing for you.

I am thinking right now of a certain man. I believe that he wants to be a Christian. He says that some day he will be. But there is an impure association in his life which he has not yet been willing to give up. Which means more to a man: adulterous pleasure while on this earth and an eternity in hell, or a life that is pure and good and useful, which at the end of the way inherits an eternal heaven? I know that there is good and bad in every one of us and the only way for us to win the victory is through the help of the Lord Jesus Christ.

Won't you today say, "I am through with it all." Won't you come and turn your life over to Jesus? He is waiting to save you and give you more happiness than you can find in a life of sin. Besides this, the judgment is waiting for you out yonder. Your sin will condemn you there. But Jesus is willing to save you today and when you get there you will find that all your sins are blotted out. Won't you take Him as your Savior right now?

Sermon 8

THOU SHALT NOT STEAL

Thou shalt not steal (Exodus 20:15).

One summer when my family and I returned from a vacation trip, we found that our house had been broken into and much of our winter clothing had been stolen. One Wednesday night when we returned from prayer meeting, we found that a window in the bedroom had been torn open and a burglar had come in and stolen several articles. "But," you say, "you are not talking to me, I have never broken into anyone's house, and I never will." Yes, but when God said, "Thou shalt not steal," the commandment involved much more than breaking into a house and stealing property.

In the sixth and seventh commandments we spoke of the sacredness of human life and personality. In the eighth commandment we shall think of human rights of ownership. This brings the matter very close to us. When you speak of a man's possessions, you strike very close to his heart. But you can steal things more valuable than property. There are many intangible things which can be stolen, and I shall speak of some of them in this message.

We note here that nine of the commandments deal with what a man is and what he does with himself — his brain, his heart, his tongue, his will. The eighth commandment is the only one that concerns property. This tells us that God is more interested in the spiritual than in the material. We are more interested in our possessions, but God's chief concern is our spiritual welfare.

I. The Right Of Ownership

We begin by saying that all things belong to God. All property is vested in Him. He created the world and all that is in it. All of it is His. We go back to the beginning and we read, "In the beginning God created the heaven and the earth." In Exodus 19:5 He said, "All the earth is mine." In I Corinthians 10:26 we read, "The earth is the Lord's, and the fulness thereof." God holds a first mortgage on everything. Suppose you build a house or a bridge or a skyscraper or an ocean liner. The wood, iron and steel you use belongs to God. The house you live in belongs to Him. The money which you claim as yours belongs to the Lord; you are just a trustee. He has entrusted you with these possessions for a short time only. If He chose to do it, He could wipe out everything you own in a second's time.

We have title companies which trace the titles of property. When you buy a piece of property, they look back through the records in order to be able to clear the title. Maybe they find that Jack Jones bought the property from John Smith. He bought it from Bill Baker. They go back until they find that the government granted this property to someone years ago. But where did the government get it? God has never transferred the right of ownership to any government under the sun.

But right here we see how gracious and wonderful God is! Though He owns everything, He loves us and lends these things to us for our enjoyment. Before I was married I did not own a car. I wanted to take my girl friend for a ride, so my older brother consented to lend me his car. One night I took the car, went after the girl, picked up some other friends and we had a good ride and an enjoyable evening.

I didn't own the car; it belonged to my brother. He simply lent it to me for my enjoyment. So it is that God owns everything, yet in His infinite love and grace He lends them to us for our enjoyment. Oh, what a wonderful Father He is, indeed!

Yes, God owns everything and we are simply His trustees. A trustee is one who holds and handles property for the benefit of another. Some years ago I served on the board of trustees of a Baptist college. This did not mean that I owned one foot of the property. It simply meant that I was chosen to help direct the activities of the college for the benefit of the owners. Life would be better for us all and our possessions would never master us if we remembered that God has simply lent them to us for a while, to be used for His glory.

But while all of this is true, mankind does have a right of ownership under God. There are some in the world who would take away this right and have everything vested in the state. When this happens human personality is belittled, God is denied, the state is supreme, and man becomes a slave instead of a free being. Communism and socialism have their roots in atheism. In such societies there is no room for God, and man loses his position as one who is loved by a Supreme Being. Man becomes a machine and nothing else. The right to own property under God is certainly proved by the Scriptures. We read that "every good gift and every perfect gift . . . cometh down from the Father." God's greatest men in the Bible owned property—Abraham, David and Solomon. The children of Israel inherited the Promised Land and the property was divided among them.

This commandment emphasizes the dignity of ownership. In the beginning of the world, God gave Adam the right to have dominion over every living thing. That dominion carries with it rights of ownership. The man who owns something has a bigger stake in society and is a better man for it. In ancient Rome a mob rushed through the streets, crying out for more food and better entertainment. It was a mob which owned nothing. A man is always a better citizen and more contented when he owns something.

So we can easily see the reason for this commandment. God is simply saying that it is perfectly all right for men to own property, and that it is wrong to take from that man the property which belongs to him. Do you own a house, a car, a business, stocks and bonds? Then under God they are yours. It is wrong in God's sight for another person to take them. Since our human laws are based on the divine law, it is also wrong in the sight of man for one to take that which belongs to another. So we hear God thundering from Sinai so loudly that all generations can hear Him, "Thou shalt not steal."

II. THE RIGHT OF OWNERSHIP VIOLATED

How do we rob others?

1. *There is the theft of property.* This is the most common type of theft, but is not the only type. There are three ways to gain property — by gift, by work, or by theft. The first two are lawful; the third is unlawful. If somebody loves you and gives you property you become the owner of that property. If you work hard and earn property, you become the owner. But the man who steals in any way is guilty before God and a menace to mankind.

You can rob by direct seizure. This includes a man who robs a bank, who breaks into your home, or who seizes your property. It includes a man who embezzles fifty thousand dollars from his employer and flees to a foreign country.

If I have ten dollars and you steal it, I have lost ten dollars. But you have lost much more. You have lost your self-respect; you know yourself as a thief and you suffer all the penalties that come to a thief. A girl in college stole money and jewelry from the other girls in the dormitory. The officials searched her room, found the stolen property and she was sent home in disgrace. The other girls lost some jewelry and a few dollars; she lost everything. There is an old saying that honesty is the best policy. For the Christian it ought to be more than a policy; it ought to be the very heart of his Christianity.

But someone will say, "Yes, but one has to live," and gives this as an excuse for dishonest dealings. No, you don't have to live, but you do have to be honest. I would rather be honest and die and face God with clean hands, than to live and be a thief. But you won't die if you are honest. God will take care of you. He never fails.

While we are thinking of direct theft, let us remember that a small theft makes you guilty just the same as a large one. I am thinking now of a traveling man whom I knew in other days. He went to church and prayer meeting wherever he happened to be on Sunday or Wednesday night. He knew all the pastors and churches in his part of the country; he would not think of stealing a dollar. Yet his bathroom was filled with towels from many hotels. I believe that he had broken this commandment.

You can steal from others by fraud. Today there are too many compromises in the matter of honesty. Life offers a hundred ways to be dishonest, little ways which will not cause you to go to jail, little ways whereby you can still be respectable in the sight of others. Here is where the real temptations lie for most of us. You are not tempted to rob a bank or steal from a cash register. But there are so many border line cases which compromise our honesty.

Several years ago a picture on the front cover of the *Satur-*

day Evening Post showed a nice old lady buying a Thanks-giving turkey from a fat, friendly butcher. The turkey was being weighed on the butcher's scales. He stood on one side of the counter and the nice old lady stood on the other side of the counter. Their eyes were both riveted on the weight indicator and you could see an expression of delight in the eyes of each of them. Cautiously the butcher had placed his big right thumb on the scales, pressing down. On the other side the sweet old lady had placed her chubby forefinger underneath the scales, pressing upward. Each one was unaware of the other's deception. Each one was trying to take advantage of the other.

God's Book has something to say about weights and measures. "Thou shalt not have in thy bag divers weights, a great and a small. Thou shalt not have in thine house divers measures, a great and small. But thou shalt have a perfect and just weight, a perfect and just measure shalt thou have: that thy days may be lengthened in the land which the Lord thy God giveth thee" (Deut. 25:13-15).

Business men have many practices today which are far from honest. They say, "Business is business." They excuse themselves by saying, "They all do it." Some years ago I traded in an old car for a new one. The speedometer on the old car showed that it had been run 48,000 miles. A few days later a man called me and said, "I am thinking of buying your old car from the dealer. I notice that the speedometer shows that it has been run 32,000 miles. Is this correct?" The dealer had turned the speedometer back 16,000 miles. The service manager of one automobile company told me that nearly every dealer in that city observed this same practice. But that doesn't make it right—that is a violation of this commandment.

There is an illustration in Proverbs 20:14: "It is naught, it is naught, saith the buyer: but when he is gone his way, then he boasteth." Here is the way it works. A man wants to sell a house, we will say. The real estate dealer looks it over and finds a thousand things wrong with it. He runs the price down $1500 and buys the property. After the deal is made he says, "Ha, ha! I surely put one over on him. The house is worth much more than I paid for it." He has violated this commandment.

Or here is a mother who gets on the bus with her child. She wants to save a few pennies so she lies about the child's age and pays only half fare. She chuckles over what she has done. The bus company will not go broke because of this transaction, but look what has happened. The mother has lied and cheated in front of the child, and is building up dishonesty in that child. Someday she will wonder why the child goes wrong.

A man was employed to build a massive arch on the campus of Leland Stanford University. Instead of filling the center of the columns with expensive concrete, he filled them with rubbish and building debris. One day an earthquake shook that section of the state and the arch fell in ruins. The man's dishonest act was revealed to the world. Dishonesty never pays. "Be sure your sin will find you out."

Another way to violate this commandment is by gambling. God's principle is that we obtain what we need by working for it. But the gambler wants to get something for nothing. So we have all sorts of gambling all over the country. Our annual gambling bill runs over six billion dollars, and it is the poor man who usually suffers. He is the one who spends money before he earns it, he is the one who causes his family to suffer, he is the one who embezzles his employer's money and gambles it away.

Gambling grapples its victims with hooks of steel. It gets a more tenacious grip on a man than whiskey or dope. It is difficult for a man ever to get loose from this habit. Though a man has lost thousands of dollars, he will spend even the grocery money or the rent money, hoping to get something for nothing. The thief and the gambler are twin brothers. They both pride themselves on outsmarting someone else. They both are trying to get without working that which someone else has gotten by the sweat of his brow.

But one of the vilest forms of robbery is failure to pay our just debts. I am thinking of a church man who owed many people in the town where he lived. When he would get a little money he would go on a trip and let his creditors wait. He was violating this commandment. Of all the people who ought to pay their debts, the Christian should stand in the front line. Many people judge Christ, the Church and Christianity by the way that we pay our debts.

The Christian who is strictly honest removes the reproach of the world. Here is a man who is supposed to be a Christian. His grocer is not a Christian. When this Christian fails to pay his grocery bill, his actions become a reproach to Christianity. You can never make that grocer feel that there is anything to Christianity. The outside world does not read the Bible, but it reads our lives. If we are not honest, we will never win anybody.

When the Welsh Revival was at its height, thousands of people were being saved. A certain merchant said, "There is nothing to this revival." But soon his old customers came in and began paying their overdue bills. Then he said, "There must be something to a revival which would make men pay their old debts." Consequently he went to church and found Christ as his Savior.

One day Jesus came to Jericho. In the town there was a little, old, stingy, grasping Jew who made his living by collecting taxes for the Roman government and by keeping a big slice for himself. When he heard that Jesus was coming, he climbed up in a sycamore tree to see Him. Jesus stopped under that tree and said, "Zacchaeus, come down; for today I must abide at thy house." Zacchaeus climbed down the tree and received Jesus gladly. How do we know that Zacchaeus was saved? We know it because of his changed attitude. This is what he said, "The half of my goods give I to the poor; and if I have taken any thing from any man by false accusation, I restore him fourfold." From then on I believe that the people of Jericho had some confidence in his religion. But they won't have any in yours if you don't pay your debts. They know that you are violating the eighth commandment.

2. *There is the theft of a person.* Every man has a right to be free. Any slavery which takes away that freedom is stealing. In the last few years, there have been many kidnaping cases in America. This is the worst kind of stealing. Not only is the child stolen from its parents, but happiness and peace of mind are also stolen.

3. *There is the theft of purity.* Some low-down scoundrel goes with an innocent girl and causes her to fall in love with him. Because of her infatuation for him, she will do anything he asks. He seduces her, robs her of her virtue, starts her on the downward path and often ruins her whole life. That is theft of the basest and meanest sort. Let me advise young people not to go far enough to get yourself into such a dangerous position.

4. *There is the theft of peace and happiness.* Here is where we rob by our neglect. In the olden days a famous author gave very little time and affection to his faithful wife. Soon she pined away and died. He read her diary and learned how she had yearned for his affection and attention. It broke his heart. Going out to the cemetery he threw himself upon her grave and cried out, "I loved you. Don't you hear me, I did love

you." But it was too late. He had robbed her of the happiness which he could have given her. Oh, we ought to bring our flowers to people while they are living.

There are some who steal domestic happiness. A man or woman goes into a happy family, uses all the charm at their command, steals the affection of a husband or wife, breaks up a home and hurts all concerned. David did this. While Uriah was away in battle, David took Uriah's wife. He stole her for himself. When Uriah came home, he was broken-hearted. David followed up this sin by another sin. He sent Uriah to the front line of the battle where he was sure to be killed. He added the sin of murder to the sin of theft and adultery. God punished him severely for it. There is too much of this same thing going on today. God will not hold you guiltless if you violate His commandment in this way.

Employers often rob employees. "Behold, the hire of the labourers . . . which is of you kept back by fraud, crieth: and the cries . . . are entered into the ears of the Lord" (Jas. 5:4). I once knew a man who was acclaimed abroad for his great gifts to charity and religion. Yet I knew some of his employees and they had been working for him for years for starvation wages.

Employees can also rob employers. They do so by not giving a fair day's work for a fair day's wage. I believe that the Capital and Labor issue should be settled in a Christian way. The employer should say, "I have a business here, and I need your help. I will pay you well and give you good working conditions and not try to get everything for myself." Then the employee should say, "Unless my boss prospers, I will not have a job. I will give him a good day's work and look out for his interests and trust him to look out for mine."

5. *There is the theft of reputation.* You hear something which is detrimental to a man's good name. You don't investi-

gate to see whether it is true or not, but you repeat it to others. Soon the story is going the rounds and a good name has been stolen. Shakespeare said, "Who steals my purse steals trash, but he that filches from me my good name, robs me of that which not enriches him, and makes me poor indeed." That is highway robbery at its blackest. It is better to steal a man's money than his good name. A gossiper is indeed a thief. Do you know a choice morsel of gossip about someone? Then swallow it. Never repeat it, whether it is true or not. In so doing you may save someone from heartbreaking sorrow.

6. *There is the theft of character*. In the olden days the Indians made their prisoners "run the gauntlet." The warriors would line up in two columns. The prisoner was forced to run between these two columns and as he ran, each warrior would strike him with a club. Many prisoners were killed in this way. There was very little safety there. I am thinking of the gauntlet through which our children must run. They have to run by the saloons and all the enticing things of the radio and television. What is the world doing? It is robbing many of them of a chance to build a good life. Let me tell you that in these days Christian parents need to pray and work harder than ever to keep the world from stealing the character of their children.

7. *There is the theft of faith*. The infidel Hume led his mother to embrace his atheistic beliefs. When she lay dying, he cried out, "Mother hold on." "Son," she sobbed, "I have nothing to hold on to—you have robbed me of my faith." I see a crippled man going down the street, with crutches under either arm. It would be a cruel thing if I knocked those crutches out from under his arm and caused him to fall. Yet, how much worse are the teachers and preachers who rob one of his faith, who take away his spiritual supports.

8. *There is the theft from the needy*. The Bible says, "It

is [God] that giveth thee power to get wealth." Since that is true, we owe it to God to use our money to help those who are less fortunate. We need to recognize our obligations to others. Listen to Ephesians 4:28: "Let him that stole steal no more: but rather let him labor, working with his hands the thing which is good, that he may have to give to him that needeth." We are told here that we are to work hard in order to have something to give to the needy. It is sinful to obtain money and hoard it or squander it upon ourselves. The rich man who spends fifty thousand dollars for his daughter's coming-out party is a thief; it would have been better if he had given this money to the needy.

In a recent newspaper article I read that some of the Women's Clubs of America were going to erect a cross which would cost three million dollars. Certainly this money could be used to a better advantage.

9. *There is theft from God.* The prophet Malachi asked the question, "Will a man rob God?" Then the answer comes, and God says, "Ye have robbed me . . . in tithes and offerings." It is grand larceny to steal from God. "The love of money is the root of all [kinds of] evil." The greatest evil about money is connected with stealing from God. You condemn your neighbor for not paying his debts. God has a right to condemn you if you are taking part of His money. What caused the tragic death of Ananias and Sapphira? Simply this—they didn't pay God what they promised to pay Him.

Your church is busy twenty-four hours a day at the task of winning the lost. We do that at home through our efforts here, and abroad through our missionaries. When you withhold your tithe, you are withholding the Gospel from those who know not a Savior. "But," you say, "I must pay my debts." We owe God the first debt. If we are willing to pay that, He will help us pay what we owe. I never saw a tither who didn't pay his debts. We pay taxes for the privilege of living in a great country; let us pay tithes for the privilege of enjoying a great salvation.

III. The Remedy For Stealing

The same remedy applies here as to all sin — that is to have Jesus Christ in your heart. He can cleanse all sin and give you power to overcome.

Before he was saved Bishop Arthur Moore of the Methodist Church was a railroad man. I heard him preach when I was a boy. He said that when he found Christ as his Savior, he felt compelled to restore to the railroad company the value of certain things which he had taken from them. That is what Jesus Christ can do for a man.

One day a man came to Mr. Moody and said, "I have taken $1,500 from my employers. I want to become a Christian. What must I do?" Mr. Moody asked him if he had any of the money left. The man replied, "I have $950 left. Can't I go into business with that and make enough money to pay back that which I have taken?" Mr. Moody said, "This money is not yours. You must return the $950 to your employer." "But I may be put into prison," said the man. Mr. Moody said, "That does not matter. You must do the right thing. Go and confess your sin and give the money back to your employer." The man promised to do this. Mr. Moody went along with him. The man told his story, returned the $950 and promised to pay the balance. The eyes of his two employers filled with tears and they said, "We will gladly forgive you, and give you time to pay back the balance." There in the office the four men went down on their knees and prayed. Restitution was made, a soul was saved and this man later became an officer in the firm.

If men will forgive us our trespasses, surely Christ will forgive if we come to Him. A dying man said, "My record is clean and the road ahead is clear." God help us all to be able to say that.

Charles G. Finney was holding a meeting in a certain place and a man came forward to the altar, saying that he wanted to be saved. Mr. Finney knelt and prayed with him. "Lord," he prayed, "here is a man who wants to give thee his whole heart." And the man said, "Amen." "Lord," he prayed, "here is a man who wants to share his home with you." And the man again said, "Amen." "Lord," he prayed again, "here is a man who wants to share his business with you. He wants you to come in as a partner and help him conduct his business." Then the man was strangely quiet, and Mr. Finney said, "Why don't you say 'Amen'?" The man said, "Because, I am not ready to take Christ into my business and share it with Him and have Him help me conduct it."

Oh, foolish man! And I would say the same thing to anyone who is not willing to let Jesus come in and help in every area of life. Give your heart to Him. Let Him reign on the throne of your life. Then life will be better for you in a thousand million ways.

Sermon 9

THOU SHALT NOT BEAR FALSE WITNESS

Thou shalt not bear false witness against thy neighbour (Exodus 20:16).

God made all the creatures of the world, including man, whom He made in His own image. He gave man one gift which no other creature has, a gift which distinguishes him from the brute. He gave him the power of speech. Now speech is sometimes used to gladden the heart. When the lover says to his beloved, "I love you," that gladdens the heart. When the jury foreman says, "Not guilty," that gladdens the defendant's heart. When the doctor says, "I have made a thorough examination and find no malignancy"; when the boss says, "I am going to raise your salary"; when the mother-in-law, after a long visit, says, "I am going home"; these all gladden the heart.

But speech is sometimes used to sadden the heart. When the doctor says, "I am sorry, but it is cancer"; when the telegram says, "Your loved one has died"; when the boss says, "You are fired"; when the broker says, "You have lost all your money"; when someone calls and says, "Your son is in trouble" — these all sadden the heart. But the greatest and grandest use of speech is used to tell someone of Jesus, who died to save from sin and to give eternal life.

The worst use of speech is to use it in telling a lie. God is the God of truth, the author of truth. We are made in

His image, so our lives should reflect the truth of God. A lie in any form is strictly ungodly. Truth is the foundation of the Church, the home, and the social order. A lie disintegrates and destroys the foundation. The Devil uses the lie as his chief weapon to fight God and destroy man. And yet, lying is one of the most common sins of our age. Christians as well as non-Christians are guilty.

There is an old Jewish legend which says that when Noah was ushering the animals into the ark just before the flood, falsehood came up in the form of a lizard. Noah said in effect, "Those who enter must go into the ark in pairs." So falsehood went away, secured sin as his mate, and they entered into the ark together. Ever since that day lying and sin have never been separated — they are always together. Men lie when they sin and sin when they lie. Some people look with horror upon the outward sins of the flesh, yet they are not careful about their speech. They often lie, they often bear false witness. God puts this down as a lie. So He gives us the ninth commandment, "Thou shalt not bear false witness against thy neighbour."

But who is our neighbor? Jesus, in the story of the Good Samaritan, tells us that every soul in the world is our neighbor. His property may not join ours on the right or the left, but it does join at the center of the earth. Every man is our neighbor, and we sin if we lie about anybody.

I. THE BIBLE'S MESSAGE ABOUT LYING

The conflict of the ages is the conflict between Satan and Christ. This is illustrated in the matter of lying. In John 8:44 we are told that Satan is a liar and the father of lies. In John 14:6 we are told that Christ is the truth. So we see that down through the ages it is Christ versus Satan — the truth versus a lie. Now where do you stand in this conflict?

Whose side are you on? You can follow Christ and the truth or Satan and lying. The words that you speak tell the world where you stand. "Out of the abundance of the heart, the mouth speaketh" (Matt. 12:34).

Our words reveal our inward nature. Jesus was perfectly right in heart, so all the words that He spoke are perfectly right. People judge us by our words, as they judged Peter when he denied Christ. If our speech is true and pure and clean, the world will know that we have something of the nature of Christ in us.

Look at what the Bible says about our words.

> *Psalm 19:14:* Let the words of my mouth, and the meditation of my heart, be acceptable in thy sight, O Lord, my strength, and my redeemer.
>
> *Psalm 141:3:* Set a watch, O Lord, before my mouth; keep the door of my lips.
>
> *Proverbs 10:11:* The mouth of a righteous man is a well of life.
>
> *Proverbs 16:24:* Pleasant words are as an honeycomb, sweet to the soul, and health to the bones.
>
> *Proverbs 25:11:* A word fitly spoken is like apples of gold in pictures of silver.
>
> *Psalm 120:2:* Deliver my soul, O Lord, from lying lips, and from a deceitful tongue.
>
> *Matthew 12:37:* For by thy words thou shalt be justified, and by thy words thou shalt be condemned.
>
> *Ephesians 4:25:* Wherefore putting away lying, speak every man truth with his neigbour; for we are members one of another.

All the sin and trouble in the world began with lying. God told Adam and Eve that death would come upon them if they ate of the fruit of a certain tree. The Devil came up and said to Eve, "Come on, eat of this fruit," but Eve replied, "No, God said if we ate of that tree we would die."

But Satan said, "You are not going to die. Everything is all right; go ahead and eat the fruit." Well, Eve and Adam believed the Devil's lie instead of the Word of Almighty God. They partook of the fruit and sin entered into the world. Satan's lie brought on all of our troubles. All wars, sickness, death and sorrow stem from the fact that our first parents believed a lie.

What was it that put Jesus to death? It was a bunch of lies. He lived a perfect life; He went about doing good. Then His jealous and slanderous enemies got together and took counsel how they might kill Him. How did they carry out the plan? They hired false witnesses to go before the court and lie about Him, and because of these lies, He was finally condemned and crucified. No wonder God hates a lie. Lying brought all the sin and trouble into the world, it brought His Only-begotten Son to His death. So the Bible speaks out, "Thou shalt not bear false witness against thy neighbour."

II. VIOLATIONS OF THIS COMMANDMENT

1. *It is violated in courts of justice.* Our courts are established for the execution of justice. Justice is based on truth. Therefore all testimony before a court must be truthful and dependable. A false witness may defeat the ends of justice. If a man lies on the witness stand, he may rob another man of his property, of his time, or of his life. So you see that a false witness is a liar and may also be a thief or a murderer.

2. *It is violated by direct lies.* What is lying? The dictionary tells us that it is any species of designed deception. If you try to make an impression contrary to the plain truth, you lie. And today, in every walk of life, men are guilty of direct lying. When you deliberately decide to deceive another person in any way, that is lying.

Some people think that it is all right to tell a white lie. I don't believe there is any such thing in God's sight. It is either the truth or it isn't the truth. But someone says, "We have to do a little bit of lying today in business, or starve." All right, then it would be better to starve. It is better to live on God's side and die than to be on the Devil's side and live. But I don't believe you are forced to lie or exaggerate in order to get along. I believe what Jesus says, "Seek ye first the kingdom of God, and his righteousness; and all these things shall be added unto you."

God's nature doesn't change. It is the same today as when He gave the commandments at Sinai. He is not going to change His nature to accommodate present business practices. God hated deception thousands of years ago, and He hates it today. "Lying lips are an abomination to the Lord. . . . he that speaketh lies shall not escape" (Prov. 12:22; 19:5). You may escape for a little while, but in time God will pay off.

3. *It is violated by gossip and slander.* We are told that a scorpion carries his poison in his tail and a snake carries his poison back of his cheek. The slanderer and gossiper carries his poison in his tongue. This poison begins in an evil heart and comes up through the tongue. There are some who would never kill anybody with a pistol, but they don't hesitate to destroy people with the tongue. In God's sight one is just as bad as the other. Not many of us are rich, nor do we have great houses, nor stores, nor stocks and bonds. But through the years we have built a good name in the community, and if you tear that name down with your slander, we have nothing left.

"Come and let us smite him with the tongue" (Jer. 18:18). Many people enjoy doing that. Some smite over the telephone and some over the back fence. But the worst type of smiters I have known are those who gather outside the church just before or after some service, and who try to destroy God's servant and God's work. In a certain church a few people were trying to hurt the preacher. They were slandering him and trying to line up others to help them in their dirty work. When they went to one deacon, he replied, "I'll never be a party to anything that destroys a man." He remembered that God had said, "Touch not mine anointed, and do my prophets no harm." Any day laborer can tear down an old building, but it takes a skilled man to build a cathedral or a church. Anyone can tear down character; it takes a real Christian to build it.

The Devil has some servants whom he values very highly. I wonder if any of them suit his purpose as well as a slanderer or a gossiper. In a museum in Venice there is a machine which one of the tyrants of old used to shoot poisoned arrows into those whom he hated. Today many people have the same kind of machine, but it is called the tongue. They use it to shoot the poison of slander into their innocent victims.

Dr. W. B. Riley tells of a man who, when he was boarding a ship, felt a sharp sting in his back. He paid no attention to it. A few minutes later he found that an enemy had shot a tiny lance with a poison tip into his back. In a little while he was dead. But that is nothing compared to the injury which you can inflict by the wrong use of the tongue.

The heart of the Christian religion is love. Before speaking ill of anyone you ought to think of them in terms of love. You ought to remember your own failings and remember how easily you can hurt someone else — then keep silent. It may give you a certain satisfaction to discuss the weaknesses of others, but this will not elevate your soul or enrich you spiritually. If a real Christian slanders someone else, he soon gets a feeling of uncleanness and wishes for some place where he might wash his soul. Can you imagine Jesus gossiping with James and John about the other disciples? Of course not. And certainly we should take Him as our example.

You remember the old verse:

There is so much bad in the best of us,
And so much good in the worst of us,
That it hardly behooves any of us,
To talk about the rest of us.

A group of men were talking together and something bad was brought up against another man. One man in the group said, "I don't believe it. Let's trace it down." They did trace it down and found out that it was a lie. Then they formed the T.I.D. Club. From that time on they traced things down instead of gossiping, which usually means lying. Up in New York City a group of girls in a department store formed a club known as "The Doorkeeper's Circle." When asked why they chose that name, they said it was because their motto was, "Keep thou the door of my mouth."

A certain church had just secured a new pastor. One day a gossiping woman said to an eager listener, "The preacher's wife went to the meeting and he came into the room in anger and took her out." The preacher answered by saying, "There are four things I would like to say about this. First, I never interfere with my wife's choices. Second, my wife never attended that meeting. Third, I did not force my wife to go home. Fourth, I don't even have a wife." All gossip should be submitted to the test of reason. A certain man once said that if he had his way the slanderer would be hung by his tongue and those who listened to him would be hung by the ears.

Surely you remember the old story of the woman who gossiped about her pastor. But she was a real Christian, so she went to the pastor and apologized to him. Then he said, "I forgive you all right, but I want you to do something for me." She readily agreed to do anything he asked. He gave her a basket of feathers and told her to go to each corner in the community and throw out a handful of these feathers into the wind. When she had done this, she came back to him and reported that the task was completed. "No," said the preacher, "you must now go out and gather all of those feathers up again." "But," she said, "that would be impossible." Then he taught her the lesson that when slander has been spread abroad, it can never be recalled.

The doctors today can cure many diseases, but no doctor can heal the wounds caused by a slanderous tongue. No surgeon can cut out the poison which has entered the bloodstream of an innocent victim. Let's be careful about what we say of others. Let us speak in love always. Extreme slander is punishable by law, but many cases never reach the court. However, these cases will not escape the judgment of God.

4. *It is violated by evil insinuations.* There are some things which do not come under the head of slander, but they can be just as dangerous. You don't actually accuse someone of evil, you just insinuate, you just suggest that it might be so. In so doing you often seriously injure one about whom you are talking.

5. *It is violated by fulsome flattery.* I am not talking about a just and honest compliment. All of us like to be complimented. The machinery of the world would run much smoother, if it were lubricated by the oil of appreciation. But gushing flattery and insincere praise come under the head of lies. The Bible tells us that some people speak

with flattering lips and a double heart. In other words, the heart does not mean what the lips say; there is no sincerity in the speech.

Man often flatters to further his own selfish ends. He lies in using "gushy" language to gain favor for himself. Psalm 55:21 described such a man. "The words of his mouth were smoother than butter, but war was in his heart: his words were softer than oil, yet were they drawn swords." We ought to praise people, but we should always be sincere about it. If you are not sincere, the Bible calls your insincerity lying.

6. *It is violated sometimes when we remain silent.* There is such a thing as talking too much, and there is such a thing as failing to speak up when we should. If your neighbor is accused of some evil and you know he is innocent, yet remain silent, you have borne false witness against him. When anyone's reputation is at stake, we ought to have the courage to speak up.

7. *It is violated by faultfinding and unjust criticism.* Jesus said, "Judge not, that ye be not judged." This does not mean that we are forbidden to form an opinion about other people. It does mean that we are not to judge bitterly nor condemn harshly in the spirit of maliciousness. We are never neutral; we always form opinions and appraise human actions. But we are not to spout out thoughtlessly our criticism and faultfinding of anyone.

One reason we find fault and criticize is that we don't know all the facts in the case. There is an old story which illustrates this truth. A certain man in a Pullman car was not able to sleep, because a little baby for whom another man was caring kept on crying. The first man blazed out, "Why don't you take that baby to its mother, so the rest of us can get some sleep." "Friend," said the man, "I wish

I could. But my wife, the baby's mother, died yesterday. Her body is in the baggage car ahead and we are taking her back to her old home for burial." Immediately the other man was sorry. He got out of his berth and took care of the little baby so that the heartbroken father could get some rest. Yes, if we understood all the circumstances, if we knew the burdens that others were bearing, we would not be so critical.

The trouble with so many of us is that we look for the worst in others, instead of the best. When a vulture flies over the field, what does he see? Probably a dead animal under a bush. But this doesn't mean that this is all there is to be seen in the field. There may be many beautiful flowers and trees there, but the vulture misses all of this, because he is looking only for something rotten. Too many people are the same way. They are not looking for the good in others — they are just looking for something bad. And when they find it, they don't hesitate to talk about it. It is not our place to judge others, to be forever critical and fault-finding. Let God be the judge. His judgments are always righteous and true. In due time He will reward every man according to his works.

8. *It is violated by hypocrisy*. This means lying with the life. Many of you may not lie with your lips, but the way you are living is a lie. Your life gives a lie to your profession of religion. You have joined the church and taken the name of Christian, but you are not living a Christian life. Your actions during the week give a lie to the faith which you profess on Sunday.

Billy Graham tells of being in a certain hotel with his wife one Sunday night after an extremely hard day. A convention was going on in the city and a number of delegates were in the big room next door to his room. These delegates were drinking and singing and yelling and throwing their whiskey bottles around. The Grahams couldn't possibly sleep. At two o'clock Billy said that he couldn't stand it any longer. He put on his robe and went over and knocked on the door. A man opened the door and invited him inside. As he stepped into the room another man staggered up to him and said, "What do you want?" He replied, "Can't you folks be quiet . . . we are trying to get a little rest." "Aw, come on," said the fellow, "come and have a drink." "No," said Billy, "I am a minister of the Gospel." The man clapped his hands and said, "Be quiet everybody. Here is a preacher and he wants to preach to us." Billy decided that they needed some preaching. He said to them, "Here you are away from home, drinking and carousing. Surely some of you are church members. Your pastor would be ashamed if he knew what you are doing tonight. I know God is ashamed of you." A woman in the room spoke up and said, "That is right, preacher, I am ashamed of myself. I am a Sunday-school teacher back home."

Oh, my friends, don't live a lie. Resolve in your heart that since you are a Christian you are going to live a Christian life.

9. *It is violated by lying to God.* One day you came down the aisle of the church and gave your heart to Christ. You promised to be faithful to the church and to live for the Lord. But you haven't done it. You promised to tithe and when you received your income you spent it all upon yourself, and forgot your pledge. You lied to God. I am thinking of a certain man who on Sunday morning walked down the aisle of our church to rededicate his life to the Lord. He promised that he would be faithful from that day forward. But he didn't come back to church for months. On another Sunday morning about a year later, he came down

again to make another rededication. It didn't mean a thing. His life was not changed; he had lied to God.

On the first Sunday in the New Year a man said to me after the morning service, "Preacher, that was a great service, and I am going to be here every Sunday. I promised the Lord that I would live better and be more faithful." The man never came back; he had lied to God.

These are some of the ways in which men lie, in which they bear false witness and break the ninth commandment. By breaking this commandment they hurt others, they bring reproach upon the cause of Christ, they soil their own souls, and they lose their Christian influence.

But this isn't all. The Bible tells us that all liars shall have their part in the lake of fire. This does not mean that every man who tells a lie is going to hell. If that were true, none of us would ever get to heaven. But if you continue the sin of lying, if you lock Christ out of your heart, at the end of the way, you will find yourself sinking into hell, there to spend the endless ages in intense suffering and with the vilest companions.

Now what is the remedy for this sin? What is the thing which will clean up a man's speech? There is only one remedy for this sin and all sins—Christ in the heart! You can never overcome this sin in your own strength. He alone can cleanse your heart and set you free and give you everlasting life.

But, you know, the Devil is the biggest liar of all. He tells you that you can get away with sin. God tells you that you can't, either in this world or in the world to come. The experience of millions tells us that you can't get away with sin. The Devil tells another lie. He tells you that it is all right to be a Christian, but you have plenty of time in which to make your decision. He is a liar. We know not when the hour of death will slip up on us, when every opportunity to be saved will be cut off. "Boast not thyself of tomorrow, for thou knowest not what a day will bring forth."

I have been talking about the use of the tongue. The best way I can employ mine is to tell you that Jesus is a wonderful Savior, that He can save you now, that He can transform your life now, and that He can set your feet today upon the pathway of eternal life.

A Christian man went to a saloon to give out religious tracts. He was hoping that he could help some of those who frequented this place of sin. As he came out of the saloon, a fine young man came in for a drink. This Christian man went up to him, put his hands on his shoulders, and said, "God can bless you young man." The spirit of God took this sentence and blessed it to the salvation of this young man. In later years he became a preacher and went out to tell others the wonderful story of Jesus and His love.

Oh, friends, I would come to you today, to you who are lost in sin, to you who are unhappy in this life, to you who are on the road to hell in the next life, to tell you that God wants to save and bless and use you. Won't you open up your heart and let Jesus come in? You will never, never regret it. You will thank God throughout all eternity that you trusted Christ as your Savior.

Sermon 10

THOU SHALT NOT COVET

> Thou shalt not covet thy neighbour's house, thou shalt
> not covet thy neighbour's wife, nor his manservant, nor his
> maidservant, nor his ox, nor his ass, nor anything that is
> thy neighbour's (Exodus 20:17).

We come now to study the last of the Ten Commandments. John Wesley said, "Before I can preach grace, I
must preach law." I have tried to do that in this series of
sermons. I have discussed with you all the things involved
in each commandment, then I have told you about the
grace of God. I have told you that although you have broken
these laws, Christ is the remedy for every sin and He is
always waiting to forgive, save and bless. The Ten Commandments have been like a mirror. We have held them
up before our face and we have seen ourselves as sinners,
since we have broken one or more of these commandments.
The true intent of the law was to condemn men, to show
their guilty condition before God. As we look into the law,
we see that we have fallen short of the glory of God and
in our heart we stand condemned before God.

The tenth commandment, in a certain way, sums up all
the others. Yet, in fact, it is different from all others. The
other commandments are concerned with visible acts. The
tenth commandment is concerned with inward desires. The
other commandments forbid the act of sin — this command-

ment forbids the desire to sin. If we keep this commandment perfectly, if we can keep our desires pure and good, it will not be so hard for us to keep the other commandments.

Selfishness is the root of all sin. It springs from our wrong desires. The Devil's doctrine is, "Get all you can for yourself, no matter whom it hurts." Christ's doctrine is, "Say no to yourself and follow Me." No officer of the law can enforce this commandment, for its violation is something that the human eye cannot see. It lies deep in a man's heart, where only God can see it.

Spurgeon, the great English preacher, saw thousands of people converted, but he said that he had never seen a covetous man converted. The trouble is that no man will ever confess to the sin of covetousness. I have heard many men confess many sins and ask God to forgive them. I have never heard a man pray, "Lord forgive me for my covetousness."

To covet means to desire that which belongs to someone else. If I look at your house or your car and say, "I wish I had a house or car like that," there is no covetousness involved. But if I say, "I wish I had your house or your car," thus depriving you of these things, I have broken the law. For the commandment plainly says, "Thou shalt not covet . . . any thing that is thy neighbour's."

A certain poet has said, "Be careful what you set your heart upon, for it surely shall be yours." And God, thinking of the sinfulness of the human heart, says in effect, Don't let your heart get set on anything which belongs to another.

I. The Bible Message on Covetousness

Luke 12:15: And he said unto them, Take heed, and beware of covetousness: for a man's life consisteth not in the abundance of the things which he possesseth.

Mark 7:21-23: For from within, out of the heart of men, proceed evil thoughts, adulteries, fornications, murders, thefts, covetousness, wickedness, deceit, lasciviousness, an evil eye, blasphemy, pride, foolishness: all these evil things come from within, and defile the man.

I Corinthians 6:9-10: Know ye not that the unrighteous shall not inherit the kingdom of God? Be not deceived: neither fornicators, nor idolaters, or adulterers, nor effeminate, nor abusers of themselves with mankind, nor thieves, nor covetous, nor drunkards, nor revilers, nor extortioners, shall inherit the kingdom of God.

Ephesians 5:5: For this we know, that no whoremonger, nor unclean person, nor covetous man, who is an idolater, hath any inheritance in the kingdom of Christ and of God.

We are told two things here. First, a covetous man is an idolater. He may not worship a graven image, but in his heart he worships some material object. Second, a covetous man will never enter heaven. Why? Because a covetous man has set his heart upon earthly things, and in order to be saved the heart must be set upon heavenly things.

Specifically what does the tenth commandment say?

(1) *You are not to covet your neighbor's house.* This means that you are not to covet any real estate which he owns.

(2) *You are not to covet your neighbor's wife.* Oh, in this day of loose morals, too much of this goes on and often leads to tragedy and heartbreak.

(3) *You are not to covet your neighbor's servants.* It is hard to get a good servant today. When some people see that you have a capable one, they covet that servant and try to steal him or her away from you.

(4) *You are not to covet your neighbor's ox or ass.* This means that you are not to covet any of his personal property.

The commandment ends by saying that "you are not to covet anything which belongs to anyone else." This covers the whole field. God does not say that it is wrong for you to wish for the better things of life, but sin comes in when you wish for that which belongs to someone else.

Listen to Paul: "For the love of money is the root of all evil: which while some coveted after, they have erred from the faith, and pierced themselves through with many sorrows" (I Tim. 6:10). He says here that the love of money is the root of all kinds of evil. How true that is. Men will lie and cheat and steal and kill because of the love of money. He further tells us that when you allow money to possess you, you will be pierced through with many sorrows.

An old picture shows the plight of a man condemned to death. He was blindfolded and led toward a precipice. On each side and behind him were soldiers with spears in their hands, with the points of these spears just touching the man's body. If the man moved to the right, to the left, or backward, his body would be pierced. He was pushed along until he came to the top of the precipice. At the bottom of the precipice stood a cart. The body of the cart was made of wood, and sharp spears were sticking up from it. The man was pushed forward until he tumbled over the precipice. The spears slashed through his head, neck, chest, arms, hands, legs and feet. A man who loves money will be pierced through with sorrows as was this poor man with spears.

Now on the opposite side Paul tells us to covet the best gifts. It is right to covet health, a good education, a good name, kindness, a sweet spirit and a Christian character. As you covet these things you strive for them and it makes you a better person. You become of more help to others and of more service to God. It is all right to covet the privilege to work; it is all right to covet the opportunity to serve God. It is all right to covet the high and holy privilege of being the best Christian possible, and to covet the chance to help others and to glorify God. But coming back to the commandment, the Bible tells us that we are not to covet something which belongs to someone else.

II. The Marks of a Covetous Man

1. *A man is covetous when his thoughts are wholly taken up with this world.* This man never thinks of God, he never reads His Bible, he never goes to church, he never prays, and he never thinks about the fact that he must meet God someday in the judgment. He gives all of his time, thought and attention to material things. The world today is full of such men. They are continually craving the things which they do not have. Their lives are spent for the things of the flesh. They never look up to God, they seemingly never have a spiritual thought, they forget that the soul must live on forever.

Maybe this covetous man does come to church on Sunday morning. But he doesn't think of the Gospel in a sweet song or a good sermon. He is thinking of his business, he is making plans for the following week, he is thinking of some trip which he is going to take. If the pastor preaches one minute after twelve o'clock this man gets so impatient that he can hardly sit still. God says, "I am holy, and I hate covetousness." But this man is thinking only of material things.

We are told that the last days of the gospel age will be like the days of Sodom and Gomorrah. People bought, they sold, they sowed, they reaped, they married and were given in marriage. Were these things wrong? Certainly not, but these people were wholly taken up with these worldly matters. It is the same way today. Men are so taken up with business and pleasure and amusements and sports and social life that they have no time for the things of the soul. "What shall it profit a man, if he shall gain the whole world; and lose his own soul?"

Judas walked with Jesus. He heard His sweet voice offering peace and salvation and forgiveness to men. But when he was offered money to betray Him, the jingle of those thirty pieces of silver sounded so loudly that the sound drowned out the sweet voice of the Savior. So today men hear every other sound in the world and they follow these things because they are not interested in Christ and everlasting life.

When the Spaniards came over to South America, and sought to conquer Peru, they sent this message to the king, "Give us gold, for we Spaniards have a disease that can only be cured by gold." Is that your disease? Are you guilty of covetousness? Are your thoughts taken up with this world only?

2. *A man is covetous when his conversation is all about this world.* Some men talk only about baseball, football, hunting and fishing. Others talk only about business, stocks and bonds. For years they never mention God or Christ or the Bible. There is something wrong with a man who talks only and always about secular things. I went to the hospital to see an unsaved man who had just undergone surgery. I talked with him for a while and then asked him if he would like me to pray for him. He replied, "I don't care. You can if you want to." That man's thoughts were never on God. All of his thoughts, all of his life and all of his speech were on the things of this world. A real Christian likes to think and talk about the goodness of God and his hope in Christ.

3. *A man is covetous when he is willing to exchange his soul for material things.* One day a fine young man came to Jesus. He was immensely wealthy, but he was not satisfied. He was hungry for something which would satisfy him in this world and give him hope for the world to come. Jesus,

in effect, said to this young man, "Young man, you must make your choice. You are in love with your money, yet you want to be saved. You must choose between God and gold, between money and your Master." Now Jesus didn't want him to give up everything and become a pauper. He just wanted him to transfer his affections from money to God. He wanted him to use the money for God instead of permitting that money to master him. The young man turned Jesus down and went away sorrowful. He was going to hold on to his possessions if it cost him his soul.

You remember the story that Jesus told of the rich farmer. God gave him such a good crop that he had to build new barns in which to store it. But all the time his soul was crying out for something better. Hear him as he tries to still the voice of his soul, "Soul, thou hast much goods laid up for many years; eat, drink, and be merry." That night God took him away in death. His soul cried out for some attention, but the man was thinking only of material things. He exchanged his soul for these things. I know men today who would like to be saved, they would like to go to heaven, but they love the things of this world: they are not willing to give them up in order to inherit eternal life.

Billy Graham says that Herman Goering's wife and daughter were Christians. His wife visited him in prison the day before he committed suicide. Goering asked her, "Do you have a message from my dear little daughter?" "Yes, Herman," replied his wife, "she told me to urge you to come to Christ so that you might meet her some day in heaven." "It is too late," said Goering, "I will have to take my chance." Years before, the time had probably come for him to make a choice. The Spirit of God had called him, but he said, "No, I am going my own way. I will live my own life the way that I want to live it." He went his way and became a great power in Germany, but he lost his soul.

4. *A man is covetous when his heart is so set on the world that he will do anything to get it.* Yes, a man looks upon something which belongs to someone else and greatly desires it. His mouth waters for it. The time comes when he is willing to do anything to get it.

Let us think for a minute on an Old Testament story. Ahab was the king. Right near his palace a good man by the name of Naboth owned a vineyard. Ahab wanted that vineyard. He offered to buy it from Naboth, but Naboth said, "I am sorry, but I can't sell my vineyard. It is an inheritance from my father." Ahab went home to bed and pouted. He would not even eat—his heart coveted that vineyard. In a few minutes his wife, Jezebel, came in and said, "What's the matter, Ahab?" And he said, "Naboth has a vineyard that I want and he will not sell it to me." "Don't worry about it a minute, Ahab, I'll get it for you." So this wicked woman went out and hired two sons of the Devil to lie about Naboth. He was brought before the elders and given an unjust trial. He was sentenced to die and was then stoned to death. Jezebel then went in to Ahab and said, "All right, honey, go ahead and take your vineyard. Naboth is dead." But that is not the end of the story. Jezebel and Ahab both met tragic deaths because of their sin. Oh, what a covetous person will do to get the things of this world. As a consequence everyone suffers.

We think again of David, the man after God's own heart. He coveted the beautiful wife of one of his soldiers. His covetousness led to his stealing her and then placing her husband in the front line of battle so that he would meet his death. He was guilty of both adultery and murder. A great sin was born out of a covetous eye. But God didn't allow this sin to go unpunished. David suffered the rest of his life because of it.

There are other Bible characters who were guilty of covetousness. Eve coveted the forbidden fruit and thus brought sin into the world. Cain coveted the acceptance which God gave Abel and consequently he murdered his brother. Lot coveted the best land and lost everything that he had. Achan coveted gold, stole the forbidden treasures, and was stoned to death. Felix hoped to gain money by holding Paul in jail and lost his own soul. Judas coveted the money bag and committed suicide. In every case, covetousness brought suffering and sometimes death.

In one of John's epistles we hear him saying to Gaius, "Beloved, I wish above all things that thou mayest prosper and be in health, even as thy soul prospereth." It is all right for you to prosper if your soul is growing along with your material prosperity. I have seen many people whose souls withered as they prospered financially. When they started out in a small way, they came to church faithfully, they gave their tithe, they lived for the Lord. Then when their income increased, they moved into a new home and soon they were forgetting God and neglecting His Church. Let me tell you that material things can really get a tight grip upon you. We need to beware of covetousness, as Jesus said.

III. COVETOUSNESS CAUSES US TO BREAK THE OTHER NINE COMMANDMENTS

1. *The first commandment tells us not to have other gods before God.* A covetous man has another god. He worships gold. He substitutes material things for God.

2. *The second commandment tells us that we are not to make any graven images and bow down before them.* So-

called civilized men will not bow down before ugly gods, but their heart does bow down before material possessions.

3. *The third commandment tells us not to take the name of the Lord in vain.* We think of Ananias and Sapphira, who coveted money and who, in the house of God, lied in the name of God and broke this commandment.

4. *The fourth commandment tells us to remember the Sabbath day, to keep it holy.* Why are our stores and amusement places wide open on Sunday? It is because of covetousness, the love of money. Men desecrate the Lord's Day purely for material gain. But six days and God are far better than seven days without God.

5. *The fifth commandment tells us to honor our fathers and mothers.* A man who covets money may go against his parents' wishes to get it. He may open a saloon or engage in some other practice which breaks their hearts.

6. *The sixth commandment tells us not to kill.* Judas loved money and that love caused him to betray the Son of God into the hands of murderers. The man who sells liquor in order to gain money, hastens the death of others. A man insures another man for a heavy sum and then kills him in order to collect the money. Covetousness has brought on murder.

7. *The seventh commandment tells us not to commit adultery.* Prostitution is one of the oldest professions in the world. It is done for money. Millions of dollars have been made and thousands of lives have been ruined as this commandment was broken. In one city the mayor and the police gave protection to the prostitutes and received a slice out of every dollar paid to these poor souls.

8. *The eighth commandment tells us that we are not to steal.* But nearly all stealing is caused by covetousness, the love of material things.

9. *The ninth commandment tells us that we are not to bear false witness.* But a man says, "If you pay me enough, I will go on the witness stand and tell such and such a lie."

So you see that if a man is covetous, if he breaks the tenth commandment, if he loves money, all of this may lead to the breaking of any or all of the other nine commandments. No wonder God brings the Decalogue to a close by saying, "Thou shalt not covet."

IV. The One Substitute for Covetousness

Instead of permitting covetousness to fill the heart, you must enthrone Christ in that heart. He is the antidote, the remedy for every sin. Oh, my friend, don't just live for this world. Don't set your affections upon the things of this life. Remember God. Remember that you must meet Him someday. Give your heart to Christ and give some time and attention to your soul.

Jesus kept every law perfectly. He was never covetous. Think about Him, the King of Kings, the Lord of Lords. He was highest in heaven. He was full of glory and honor. He was the richest of the rich. He created all things and owned all things. And what did He do? He turned His back upon it all. He gave it all up for you and me. He came down into the world, became the poorest of the poor, and suffered and bled and died that we might live forever. Oh, what a Savior He is! I urge you to turn from all sin and sinful desires and let Him fill your life with true riches.

Dr. J. Wilbur Chapman said, "Anything which dims my vision of Christ, or takes away my taste for the Bible, or cramps my prayer life, or makes Christian work difficult, is wrong for me. As a Christian, I must turn away from it."

Covetousness does all of this to the soul. We must fight it in the strength of Christ.

A certain Christian man was very poor, but he loved Christ devotedly. He was given a trip to New York City. His first day was spent in sight-seeing. When this exciting day was over, he went down upon his knees in his hotel room and said, "Lord, I want to thank Thee that I have not seen a single thing today that I want." Yes, the man who has Christ in his heart is a contented man.

It is a tragic thing to see a man work himself to death and then die and leave it all behind. You can't take it with you. Rochester said, "If Mr. Benny can't take it with him, he won't go." But Mr. Benny, like all the rest of us, must go.

Alexander the Great gave orders that when he died, his men were to cut holes in each side of the casket, and his empty hands were to be left protruding from these holes. This was to show to everyone that although he had conquered the world, he could take nothing with him into the world to come.

Out in Hollywood a group of movie people meet often for breakfast. They have various movie stars and other prominent people come and speak to them. Sometimes they heckle these speakers and whistle at them. One morning a beautiful young woman was their guest. *Look* magazine had chosen her as one of the ten most beautiful girls in America. She was making $2,000 a week as a movie star. Her picture was on the front of *Life* magazine. They asked her to say a few words, and when she came to the microphone she said, "Gentlemen, I am in love. I have just fallen in love." The crowd shouted and clapped their hands and someone cried out, "Who is the lucky guy?" And she replied, "I have just fallen in love with Jesus Christ." The crowd sat there stunned — you could hear a pin drop. Then she told them that she was giving up a promising career in the movies and that she was going to give all of her life to Christ. Later she married a young preacher and is now making preparations to go as a missionary.

This young woman, Colleen Townsend Evans, and her husband ate dinner one night in London with Billy Graham and his wife. Billy asked her the question, "Colleen, have you ever been sorry for the stand that you took?" And she replied, "I wouldn't trade places with the greatest star in Hollywood, or the Queen of England, or the President of the United States. Jesus Christ is wonderful and thrilling to me."

Oh, my friends, He can mean everything to you, too. Won't you let Him come into your heart today?

SCRIPTURE INDEX